Romulus: Founder of Rome

Romulus: Founder of Rome

Makers of History Series

Jacob Abbott

Cedar Lake Classics

Copyright © 2023 by Cedar Lake Classics

This is an annotated edition of a public domain work.

CONTENTS

	PREFACE	vii
	PHOTO INSERT	viii
1	Cadmus	1
2	Cadmus's Letters	14
3	The Story of Æneas	27
4	The Destruction of Troy	38
5	The Flight of Æneas	50
6	The Landing in Latium	65
7	Rhea Silvia	78
8	The Twins	91
9	The Founding of Rome	104
10	Organization	117
11	Wives	129
12	The Sabine War	141

CONTENTS

13 | The Conclusion 155

ABOUT JACOB ABBOTT 163
BIOGRAPHIES BY JACOB ABBOTT 165

PREFACE

IN writing the series of historical narratives to which the present work pertains, it has been the object of the author to furnish to the reading community of this country an accurate and faithful account of the lives and actions of the several personages that are made successively the subjects of the volumes, following precisely the story which has come down to us from ancient times. The writer has spared no pains to gain access in all cases to the original sources of information, and has confined himself strictly to them. The reader may, therefore, feel assured in perusing any one of these works, that the interest of it is in no degree indebted to the invention of the author. No incident, however trivial, is ever added to the original account, nor are any words even, in any case, attributed to a speaker without express authority. Whatever of interest, therefore, these stories may possess, is due solely to the facts themselves which are recorded in them, and to their being brought together in a plain, simple, and connected narrative.

The Harpies

1

Cadmus

SOME men are renowned in history on account of the extraordinary powers and capacities which they exhibited in the course of their career, or the intrinsic greatness of the deeds which they performed. Others, without having really achieved any thing in itself very great or wonderful, have become widely known to mankind by reason of the vast consequences which, in the subsequent course of events, resulted from their doings. Men of this latter class are conspicuous rather than great. From among thousands of other men equally exalted in character with themselves, they are brought out prominently to the notice of mankind only in consequence of the strong light reflected, by great events subsequently occurring, back upon the position where they happened to stand.

The celebrity of Romulus seems to be of this latter kind. He founded a city. A thousand other men have founded cities; and in doing their work have evinced perhaps as much courage, sagacity, and mental power as Romulus displayed. The city of Romulus, however, became in the end the queen and mistress of the world. It rose to so exalted a position of influence and power, and retained its ascendency so long, that now for twenty centuries every civilized nation in the western world have felt a strong interest in every thing pertaining to its history, and have been accustomed to look back with special curiosity to the circumstances of its origin. In consequence of this it has happened that though Romulus, in his actual day, performed no very great exploits, and enjoyed no preeminence above the thousand other half-savage chieftains of his class, whose names have been long forgotten, and very probably while he lived never dreamed of any extended fame, yet so brilliant is the illumination which the subsequent events of history have shed upon his position and his doings, that his name and the incidents of his life have been brought out very conspicuously to view, and attract very strongly the attention of mankind.

The history of Rome is usually made to begin with the story of Æneas. In order that the reader may understand in what light that romantic tale is to be regarded, it is necessary to premise some statements in respect to the general condition of society in ancient days, and to the nature of the strange narrations, circulated in those early periods among mankind, out of which in later ages, when the art of writing came to be introduced, learned men compiled and recorded what they termed history.

The countries which formed the shores of the Mediterranean sea were as verdant and beautiful, in those ancient days, and perhaps as fruitful and as densely populated as in modern times. The same Italy and Greece were there then as now. There were the same blue and beautiful seas, the same mountains, the same picturesque and enchanting shores, the same smiling valleys, and the same serene and genial sky. The level lands were tilled industriously by a rural population corresponding in all essential points of character with the peasantry of modern times; and shepherds and herdsmen, then as now, hunted the wild beasts, and watched their flocks and herds, on the declivities of the mountains. In a word, the appearance of the face of nature, and the performance of the great function of the social state, namely, the procuring of food and clothing for man by the artificial cultivation of animal and vegetable life, were substantially the same on the shores of the Mediterranean two thousand years ago as now. Even the plants and the animals themselves which the ancient inhabitants reared, have undergone no essential change. Their sheep and oxen and horses were the same as ours. So were their grapes, their apples, and their corn.

If, however, we leave the humbler classes and occupations of society, and turn our attention to those which represent the refinement, the cultivation, and the power, of the two respective periods, we shall find that almost all analogy fails. There was an aristocracy then as now, ruling over the widely- extended communities of peaceful agriculturalists and herdsmen, but the members of it were entirely different in their character, their tastes, their ideas, and their occupations from the classes which exercise the prerogatives of government in Europe in modern times. The nobles then were military chieftains, living in camps or in walled cities, which they built for the accommodation of themselves and their followers. These chieftains were not barbarians. They were in a certain sense cultivated and refined. They gathered around them in their camps and in their courts orators, poets, statesmen, and officers of every grade, who seem to have possessed the same energy, genius, taste, and in some respects the same scientific skill, which have in all ages and in every clime characterized the upper classes of the Caucasian race. They carried all the arts which were necessary for their purposes and plans to high perfection, and in the invention of tales, ballads and poems, to be recited at their entertainments and feasts, they evinced the most admirable taste and skill;—a taste and skill which, as they resulted not from the operation and influence of artificial rules, but from the unerring instinct of genius, have never been surpassed. In fact, the poetical inventions of those early days, far from having been produced in conformity with rules, were entirely precedent to rules, in the order of time. Rules were formed from them; for they at length became established themselves in the estimation of mankind, as models, and on their authority as models, the whole theory of rhetorical and poetical beauty now mainly reposes.

The people of those days formed no idea of a spiritual world, or of a spiritual divinity. They however imagined, that heroes of former days still continued to live and to reign in certain semi-heavenly regions among the summits of their blue and beautiful mountains, and that they were invested there with attributes in some respects divine. In addition to these divinities, the fertile fancy of those ancient times filled the earth, the air, the sea, and the sky with imaginary beings, all most graceful and beautiful in their forms, and poetical in their functions,—and made them the subjects, too, of innumerable legends and tales, as graceful, poetical, and beautiful as themselves. Every grove, and fountain, and river,—every lofty summit among the mountains, and every rock and promontory along the shores of the sea,—every cave, every valley, every water-fall, had its imaginary occupant,—the genius of the spot; so that every natural object which attracted public notice at all, was the subject of some picturesque and romantic story. In a word, nature was not explored then as now, for the purpose of ascertaining and recording cold and scientific realities,—but to be admired, and embellished, and animated;—and to be peopled, everywhere, with exquisitely beautiful, though imaginary and supernatural, life and action.

What the genius of imagination and romance did thus in ancient times with the scenery of nature, it did also on the field of history. Men explored that field not at all to learn sober and actual realities, but to find something that they might embellish and adorn, and animate with supernatural and marvelous life. What the sober realities might have actually been, was of no interest or moment to them whatever. There were no scholars then as now, living in the midst of libraries, and finding constant employment, and a never-ending pleasure, in researches for the simple investigation of the truth. There was in fact no retirement, no seclusion, no study. Every thing except what related to the mere daily toil of tilling the ground bore direct relation to military expeditions, spectacles and parades; and the only field for the exercise of that kind of intellectual ability which is employed in modern times in investigating and recording historic truth, was the invention and recitation of poems, dramas and tales, to amuse great military audiences in camps or public gatherings, convened to witness shows or games, or to celebrate great religious festivals. Of course under such circumstances there would be no interest felt in truth as truth. Romance and fable would be far more serviceable for such ends than reality.

Still it is obvious that such tales as were invented to amuse for the purposes we have described, would have a deeper interest for those who listened to them, if founded in some measure upon fact, and connected in respect to the scene of their occurrence, with real localities. A prince and his court sitting at their tables in the palace or the tent, at the close of a feast, would listen with greater interest to a story that purported to be an account of the deeds and the marvelous adventures of their own ancestors, than to one that was wholly and avowedly imaginary. The inventors of these tales would of course generally choose such subjects, and their narrations would generally consist therefore rather of embellishments of actual transactions, than of inventions wholly original. Their heroes were consequently real men; the principal actions ascribed to them were real actions, and the places referred to were real localities. Thus there was a semblance of truth and reality in all these tales which added greatly to the interest of them; while there were no means of ascertaining the real truth, and thus spoiling the story by making the falsehood or improbability of it evident and glaring.

We cannot well have a better illustration of these principles than is afforded by the story of Cadmus, an adventurer who was said to have brought the knowledge of alphabetic writing into Greece from some countries farther eastward. In modern times there is a very strong interest felt in ascertaining the exact truth on this subject. The art of writing with alphabetic characters was so great an invention, and it has exerted so vast an influence on the condition and progress of mankind since it was introduced, that a very strong interest is now felt in every thing that can be ascertained as actually fact, in respect to its origin. If it were possible now to determine under what circumstances the method of representing the elements of sound by written characters was first devised, to discover who it was, that first conceived the idea, and what led him to make the attempt, what difficulties he encountered, to what purposes he first applied his invention, and to what results it led, the whole world would take a very strong interest in the revelation. The essential point, however, to be observed, is that it is the real truth in respect to the subject that the world are now interested in knowing. Were a romance writer to invent a tale in respect to the origin of writing, however ingenious and entertaining it might be in its details, it would excite in the learned world at the present day no interest whatever.

There is in fact no account at present existing in respect to the actual origin of alphabetic characters, though there is an account of the circumstances under which the art was brought into Europe from Asia, where it seems to have been originally invented. We will give the facts, first in their simple form, and then the narrative in the form in which it was related in ancient times, as embellished by the ancient story-tellers.

The facts then, as now generally understood and believed, are, that there was a certain king in some country in Africa, named Agenor, who lived about 1500 years before Christ. He had a daughter named Europa, and several sons. Among his sons was one named Cadmus. Europa was a beautiful girl, and after a time a wandering adventurer from some part of the northern shores of the Mediterranean sea, came into Africa, and was so much pleased with her that he resolved if possible, to obtain her for his wife. He did not dare to make proposals openly, and he accordingly disguised himself and mingled with the servants upon Agenor's farm. In this disguise he succeeded in making acquaintance with Europa, and finally persuaded her to elope with him. The pair accordingly fled, and crossing the Mediterranean they went to Crete, an island near the northern shores of the sea, and there they lived together.

The father, when he found that his daughter had deceived him and gone away, was very indignant, and sent Cadmus and his brothers in pursuit of her. The mother of Europa, whose name was Telephassa, though less indignant perhaps than the father, was overwhelmed with grief at the loss of her child, and determined to accompany her sons in the search. She accordingly took leave of her husband and of her native land, and set out with Cadmus and her other sons on the long journey in search of her lost child. Agenor charged his sons never to come home again unless they brought Europa with them.

Cadmus, with his mother and brothers, traveled slowly toward the northward, along the eastern shores of the Mediterranean sea, inquiring everywhere for the fugitive. They passed through Syria and Phenicia, into Asia Minor, and from Asia Minor into Greece. At length Telephassa, worn down, perhaps, by fatigue, disappointment, and grief, died. Cadmus and his brothers soon after became discouraged; and at last, weary with their wanderings, and prevented by their father's injunction from returning without Europa, they determined to settle in Greece. In attempting to establish themselves there, however, they became involved in various conflicts, first with wild beasts, and afterward with men, the natives of the land, who seemed to spring up, as it were, from the ground, to oppose them. They contrived, however, at length, by fomenting quarrels among their enemies, and taking sides with one party against the rest, to get a permanent footing in Greece, and Cadmus finally founded a city there, which he called Thebes.

In establishing the institutions and government of Thebes, and in arranging the organization of the people into a social state, Cadmus introduced among them several arts, which, in that part of the country, had been before unknown. One of these arts was the use of copper, which metal he taught his new subjects to procure from the ore obtained in mines. There were several others; but the most important of all was that he taught them sixteen letters representing elementary vocal sounds, by means of which inscriptions of words could be carved upon monuments, or upon tablets of metal or of stone.

It is not supposed that the idea of representing the elements of vocal sounds by characters originated with Cadmus, or that he invented the characters himself. He brought them with him undoubtedly, but whether from Egypt or Phenicia, can not now be known.

Such are the facts of the case, as now generally understood and believed. Let us now compare this simple narration with the romantic tale which the early story-tellers made from it. The legend, as they relate it, is as follows.

Jupiter was a prince born and bred among the summits of Mount Ida, in Crete. His father's name was Saturn. Saturn had made an agreement that he would cause all his sons to be slain, as soon as they were born. This was to appease his brother, who was his rival, and who consented that Saturn should continue to reign only on that condition.

Jupiter's mother, however, was very unwilling that her boys should be thus cruelly put to death, and she contrived to conceal three of them, and save them. The three thus preserved were brought up among the solitudes of the mountains, watched and attended by nymphs, and nursed by a goat. After they grew up, they engaged from time to time in various wars, and met with various wonderful adventures, until at length Jupiter, the oldest of them, succeeded, by means of thunderbolts which he caused to be forged for his use, in vast subterranean caverns beneath Mount Etna and Mount Vesuvius, conquered all his enemies, and became universal king. He, however, divided his empire between himself and his brothers, giving to them respectively the command of the sea and of the subterranean regions, while he reserved the earth and the heavenly regions for himself.

He established his usual abode among the mountains of Northern Greece, but he often made excursions to and fro upon the earth, appearing in various disguises, and meeting with a great number of strange and marvelous adventures. In the course of these wanderings he found his way at one time into Egypt, and to the dominions of Agenor,—and there he saw Agenor's beautiful daughter, Europa. He immediately determined to make her his bride; and to secure this object he assumed the form of a very finely shaped and beautiful bull, and in this guise joined himself to Agenor's herds of cattle. Europa soon saw him there. She was much pleased with the beauty of his form, and finding him gentle and kind in disposition, she approached him, patted his glossy neck and sides, and in other similar ways gratified the prince by marks of her admiration and pleasure. She was at length induced by some secret and magical influence which the prince exerted over her, to mount upon his back, and allow herself to be borne away. The bull ran with his burden to the shore, and plunged into the waves. He swam across the sea to Crete, and there, resuming his proper form, he made the princess his bride.

Jupiter and Europa

Agenor and Telephassa, when they found that their daughter was gone, were in great distress, and Agenor immediately determined to send his sons on an expedition in pursuit of her. The names of his sons were Cadmus, Phœnix, Cylix, Thasus, and Phineus. Cadmus, as the oldest son, was to be the director of the expedition. Telephassa, the mother, resolved to accompany them, so overwhelmed was she with affliction at the loss of her daughter. Agenor himself was almost equally oppressed with the calamity which had overwhelmed them, and he charged his sons never to come home again until they could bring Europa with them.

Telephassa and her sons wandered for a time in the countries east of the Mediterranean sea, without being able to obtain any tidings of the fugitive. At length they passed into Asia Minor, and from Asia Minor into Thrace, a country lying north of the Ægean Sea. Finding no traces of their sister in any of these countries, the sons of Agenor became discouraged, and resolved to make no farther search; and Telephassa, exhausted with anxiety and fatigue, and now overwhelmed with the thought that all hope must be finally abandoned, sank down and died.

The Journeyings of Cadmus

Cadmus and his brothers were much affected at their mother's death. They made arrangements for her burial, in a manner befitting her high rank and station, and when the funeral solemnities had been performed, Cadmus repaired to the oracle at Delphi, which was situated in the northern part of Greece, not very far from Thrace, in order that he might inquire there whether there was any thing more that he could do to recover his lost sister, and if so to learn what course he was to pursue. The oracle replied to him that he must search for his sister no more, but instead of it turn his attention wholly to the work of establishing a home and a kingdom for himself, in Greece. To this end he was to travel on in a direction indicated until he met with a cow of a certain kind, described by the oracle, and then to follow the cow wherever she might lead the way, until at length, becoming fatigued, she should stop and lie down. Upon the spot where the cow should lie down he was to build a city and make it his capital.

Cadmus obeyed these directions of the oracle. He left Delphi and went on, attended, as he had been in all his wanderings, by a troop of companions and followers, until at length in the herds of one of the people of the country, named Pelagon, he found a cow answering to the description of the oracle. Taking this cow for his guide, he followed wherever she led the way. She conducted him toward the southward and eastward for thirty or forty miles, and at length wearied apparently, by her long journey, she lay down. Cadmus knew immediately that this was the spot where his city was to stand.

He began immediately to make arrangements for the building of the city, but he determined first to offer the cow that had been his divinely appointed guide to the spot, as a sacrifice to Minerva, whom he always considered as his guardian goddess.

Near the spot where the cow lay down there was a small stream which issued from a fountain not far distant, called the fountain of Dirce. Cadmus sent some of his men to the place to obtain some water which it was necessary to use in the ceremonies of the sacrifice. It happened, however, that this fountain was a sacred one, having been consecrated to Mars,—and there was a great dragon, a son of Mars, stationed there to guard it. The men whom Cadmus sent did not return, and accordingly

Cadmus himself, after waiting a suitable time, proceeded to the spot to ascertain the cause of the delay. He found that the dragon had killed his men, and at the time when he arrived at the spot, the monster was greedily devouring the bodies. Cadmus immediately attacked the dragon and slew him, and then tore his teeth out of his head, as trophies of his victory. Minerva had assisted Cadmus in this combat, and when it was ended she directed him to plant the teeth of the dragon in the ground. Cadmus did so, and immediately a host of armed men sprung up from the place where he had planted them. Cadmus threw a stone among these armed men, when they immediately began to contend together in a desperate conflict, until at length all but five of them were slain. These five then joined themselves to Cadmus, and helped him to build his city.

He went on very successfully after this. The city which he built was Thebes, which afterward became greatly celebrated. The citadel which he erected within, he called, from his own name, Cadmia.

Such were the legends which were related in ancient poems and tales; and it is obvious that such narratives must have been composed to entertain groups of listeners whose main desire was to be excited and amused, and not to be instructed. The stories were believed, no doubt, and the faith which the hearer felt in their truth added of course very greatly to the interest which they awakened in his mind. The stories are amusing to us; but it is impossible for us to share in the deep and solemn emotion with which the ancient audiences listened to them, for we have not the power, as they had, of believing them. Such tales related in respect to the great actors on the stage in modern times, would awaken no interest, for there is too general a diffusion both of historical and philosophical knowledge to render it possible for any one to suppose them to be true. But those for whom the story of Europa was invented, had no means of knowing how wide the Mediterranean sea might be, and whether a bull might not swim across it.

They did not know but that Mars might have a dragon for a son, and that the teeth of such a dragon might not, when sown in the ground, spring up in the form of a troop of armed men. They listened therefore to the tale with an interest all the more earnest and solemn on account of the marvelousness of the recital. They repeated it word for word to one another, around their camp-fires, at their feasts, in their journeyings,—and when watching their flocks at midnight, among the solitudes of the mountains. Thus the tales were handed down from generation to generation, until at length the use of the letters of Cadmus became so far facilitated, that continuous narrations could be expressed by means of them; and then they were put permanently upon record in many forms; and were thus transmitted without any farther change to the present age.

2

Cadmus's Letters

THERE are two modes essentially distinct from each other, by which ideas may be communicated through the medium of inscriptions addressed to the eye. These two modes are, first, by symbolical, and secondly, by phonetic characters. Each of these two systems assumes, in fact, within itself, quite a variety of distinct forms, though it is only the general characteristics which distinguish the two great classes from each other, that we shall have occasion particularly to notice here.

Symbolical writing consists of characters intended severally to denote ideas or things, and not words. A good example of true symbolical writing is to be found in a certain figure often employed among the architectural decorations of churches, as an emblem of the Deity. It consists of a triangle representing the Trinity with the 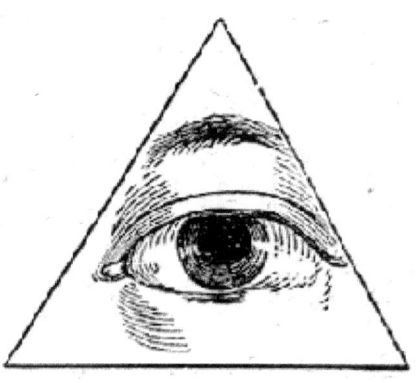 figure of an eye in the middle of it. The eye is intended to denote the divine omniscience. Such a character as this, is obviously the symbol of an idea, not the representative of a word. It may be read Jehovah, or God, or the Deity, or by any other word or phrase by which men are accustomed to denote the Supreme Being. It represents, in fine, the idea, and not any particular word by which the idea is expressed.

The first attempts of men to preserve records of facts by means of inscriptions, have, in all ages, and among all nations, been of this character. At first, the inscriptions so made were strictly pictures, in which the whole scene intended to be commemorated was represented, in rude carvings. In process of time substitutions and abridgments were adopted in lieu of full representations, and these grew at length into a system of hieroglyphical characters, some natural, and others more or less arbitrary, but all denoting ideas or things, and not the sounds of words. These characters are of the kind usually understood by the word hieroglyphics; though that word can not now with strict accuracy be applied as a distinctive appellation, since it has been ascertained in modern times that a large portion of the Egyptian hieroglyphics are of such a nature as brings them within the second of the two classes which we are here describing, that is, the several delineations represent the sounds and syllables of words, instead of being symbols of ideas or things.

It happened that in some cases in this species of writing, as used in ancient times, the characters which were employed presented in their form some natural resemblance to the thing signified, and in other cases they were wholly arbitrary. Thus, the figure of a scepter denoted a king, that of a lion, strength; and two warriors, one with a shield, and the other advancing toward the first with a bow and arrow, represented a battle. We use in fact a symbol similar to the last-mentioned one at the present day, upon maps, where we often see a character formed by two swords crossed, employed to represent a battle.

The ancient Mexicans had a mode of writing which seems to have been symbolical in its character, and their characters had, many of them at least, a natural signification. The different cities and towns were represented by drawings of such simple objects as were characteristic of them respectively; as a plant, a tree, an article of manufacture, or any other object by which the place in question was most easily and naturally to be distinguished from other places. In one of their inscriptions, for example, there was a character representing a king, and before it four heads. Each of the heads was accompanied by the symbol of the capital of a province, as above described. The meaning of the whole inscription was that in a certain tumult or insurrection the king caused the governors of the four cities to be beheaded.

But though, in this symbolical mode of writing, a great many ideas and events could be represented thus, by means of signs or symbols having a greater or less resemblance to the thing signified, yet in many cases the characters used were wholly arbitrary. They were in this respect like the character which we use to denote dollars, as a prefix to a number expressing money; for this character is a sort of symbol, that is, it represents a thing rather than a word. Our numerals, too, 1, 2, 3, &c., are in some respects of the character of symbols. That is, they stand directly for the numbers themselves, and not for the sounds of the words by which the numbers are expressed. Hence, although the people of different European nations understand them all alike, they read them, in words, very differently. The Englishman reads them by one set of words, the Spaniard by another, and the German and the Italian by others still.

The symbolical mode of writing possesses some advantages which must not be overlooked. It speaks directly to the eye, and is more full of meaning than the Phonetic method, though the meaning is necessarily more vague and indistinct, in some respects, while it is less so in others. For example, in an advertising newspaper, the simple figure of a house, or of a ship, or of a locomotive engine, at the head of an advertisement, is a sort of hieroglyphic, which says much more plainly and distinctly, and in much shorter time, than any combination of letters could do, that what follows it is an advertisement relating to a house, or a vessel, or a railroad. In the same manner, the ancient representations on monuments and columns would communicate, perhaps more rapidly and readily to the passer-by, an idea of the battles, the sieges, the marches, and the other great exploits of the monarchs whose history they were intended to record, than an inscription in words would have done.

Another advantage of the symbolical representations as used in ancient times, was that their meaning could be more readily explained, and would be more easily remembered, and so explained again, than written words. To learn to read literal writing in any language, is a work of very great labor. It is, in fact, generally found that it must be commenced early in life, or it can not be accomplished at all. An inscription, therefore, in words, on a Mexican monument, that a certain king suppressed an insurrection, and beheaded the governors of four of his provinces, would be wholly blind and unintelligible to the mass of the population of such a country; and if the learned sculptor who inscribed it, were to attempt to explain it to them, letter by letter, they would forget the beginning of the lesson before reading the end of it,—and could never be expected to attempt extending the knowledge by making known the interpretation which they had received to others in their turn. But the royal scepter, with the four heads before it, each of the heads accompanied by the appropriate symbol of the city to which the possessor of it belonged, formed a symbolical congeries which expressed its meaning at once, and very plainly, to the eye. The most ignorant and uncultivated could readily understand it. Once understanding it, too, they could never easily forget it; and they could, without any difficulty, explain it fully to others as ignorant and uncultivated as themselves.

It might seem, at first view, that a symbolical mode of writing must be more simple in its character than the system now in use, inasmuch as by that plan each idea or object would be expressed by one character alone, whereas, by our mode of writing, several characters, sometimes as many as eight or ten, are required to express a word, which word, after all, represents only one single object or idea. But notwithstanding this apparent simplicity, the system of symbolical writing proved to be, when extensively employed, extremely complicated and intricate. It is true that each idea required but one character, but the number of ideas and objects, and of words expressive of their relations to one another, is so vast, that the system of representing them by independent symbols, soon lost itself in an endless intricacy of detail. Then, besides,—

notwithstanding what has been said of the facility with which symbolical inscriptions could be interpreted,—they were, after all, extremely difficult to be understood without interpretation. An inscription once explained, the explanation was easily understood and remembered; but it was very difficult to understand one intended to express any new communication. The system was, therefore, well adapted to commemorate what was already known, but was of little service as a mode of communicating knowledge anew.

We come now to consider the second grand class of written characters, namely, the phonetic, the class which Cadmus introduced into Greece, and the one almost universally adopted among all the European nations at the present day. It is called Phonetic, from a Greek word denoting sound, because the characters which are used do not denote directly the thing itself which is signified, but the sounds made in speaking the word which signifies it. Take, for instance, the two modes   of representing a conflict between two contending armies, one by the symbolic delineation of two swords crossed, and the other by the phonetic delineation of the letters of the word battle. They are both inscriptions. The beginning of the first represents the handle of the sword, a part, as it were, of the thing signified. The beginning of the second, the letter b, represents the pressing of the lips together, by which we commence pronouncing the word. Thus the one mode is symbolical, and the other phonetic.

On considering the two methods, as exemplified in this simple instance, we shall observe that what has already been pointed out as characteristic of the two modes is here seen to be true. The idea is conveyed in the symbolical mode by one character, while by the phonetic it requires no less than six. This seems at first view to indicate a great advantage possessed by the symbolical system. But on reflection this advantage is found entirely to disappear. For the symbolical character, though it is only one, will answer for only the single idea which it denotes. Neither itself nor any of its elements will aid us in forming a symbol for any other idea; and as the ideas, objects, and relations which it is necessary to be able to express, in order to make free and full communications in any language, are from fifty to a hundred thousand, —the step which we have taken, though very simple in itself, is the beginning of a course which must lead to the most endless intricacy and complication. Whereas in the six phonetic characters of the word battle, we have elements which can be used again and again, in the expression of thousands of other ideas. In fact, as the phonetic characters which are found necessary in most languages are only about twenty-four, we have in that single word accomplished one quarter of the whole task, so far as the delineation of characters is concerned, that is necessary for expressing by writing any possible combination of ideas which human language can convey.

At what time and in what manner the transition was made among the ancient nations from the symbolic to the phonetic mode of writing, is not now known. When in the flourishing periods of the Grecian and Roman states, learned men explored the literary records of the various nations of the East, writings were found in all, which were expressed in phonetic characters, and the alphabets of these characters were found to be so analogous to each other, in the names and order, and in some respects in the forms, of the letters, as to indicate strongly something like community of origin. All the attempts, however, which have been made to ascertain the origin of the system, have wholly failed, and no account of them goes farther back than to the time when Cadmus brought them from Phenicia or Egypt into Greece.

The letters which Cadmus brought were in number sixteen. The following table presents a view of his alphabet, presenting in the several columns, the letters themselves as subsequently written in Greece, the Greek names given to them, and their power as represented by the letters now in use. The forms, it will be seen, have been but little changed.

Greek letters.	Greek names.	English representatives.
A	Alpha	A
B	Beta	B
Γ	Gamma	G
Δ	Delta	D
E	Epsilon	E
I	Iota	I
Λ	Lamda	L
M	Mu	M
N	Nu	N
O	Omicron	O
Π	Pi	P
P	Rho	R
Σ	Sigma	S
T	Tau	T
Υ	Upsilon	U

The phonetic alphabet of Cadmus, though so vastly superior to any system of symbolical hieroglyphics, for all purposes where anything like verbal accuracy was desired, was still very slow in coming into general use. It was of course, at first, very difficult to write it, and very difficult to read it when written. There was a very great practical obstacle, too, in the way of its general introduction, in the want of any suitable materials for writing. To cut letters with a chisel and a mallet upon a surface of marble is a very slow and toilsome process. To diminish this labor the ancients contrived tables of brass, copper, lead, and sometimes of wood, and cut the inscriptions upon them by the use of various tools and implements. Still it is obvious, that by such methods as these the art of writing could only be used to an extremely limited extent, such as for brief inscriptions in registers and upon monuments, where a very few words would express all that it was necessary to record.

In process of time, however, the plan of painting the letters by means of a black dye upon a smooth surface, was introduced. The surface employed to receive these inscriptions was, at first, the skin of some animal prepared for this purpose, and the dye used for ink, was a colored liquid obtained from a certain fish. This method of writing, though in some respects more convenient than the others, was still slow, and the materials were expensive; and it was a long time before the new art was employed for any thing like continuous composition. Cadmus is supposed to have come into Greece about the year 1550 before Christ; and it was not until about 650 before Christ,—that is, nearly nine hundred years later, that the art of writing was resorted to in Greece to record laws.

The evidences that writing was very little used in any way during this long period of nine hundred years, are furnished in various allusions contained in poems and narratives that were composed during those times, and committed to writing afterward. In the poems of Homer, for instance, there is no allusion, from the beginning to the end, to any monument or tomb containing any inscription whatever; although many occasions occur in which such inscriptions would have been made, if the events described were real, and the art of writing had been generally known, or would have been imagined to be made, if the narratives were invented. In one case a ship-master takes a cargo on board, and he is represented as having to remember all the articles, instead of making a record of them. Another case still more striking is adduced. In the course of the contest around the walls of Troy, the Grecian leaders are described at one time as drawing lots to determine which of them should fight a certain Trojan champion. The lots were prepared, being made of some substance that could be marked, and when ready, were distributed to the several leaders. Each one of the leaders then marked his lot in some way, taking care to remember what character he had made upon it. The lots were then all put into a helmet, and the helmet was given to a herald, who was to shake it about in such a manner, if possible, as to throw out one of the lots and leave the others in. The leader whose lot it was that should be thus shaken out, was to be considered as the one designated by the decision, to fight the Trojan champion.

Now, in executing this plan, the herald, when he had shaken out a lot, and had taken it up from the ground, is represented, in the narrative, as not knowing whose it was, and as carrying it around, accordingly, to all the different leaders, to find the one who could recognize it as his own. A certain chief named Ajax recognized it, and in this way he was designated for the combat. Now it is supposed, that if these men had been able to write, that they would have inscribed their own names upon the lots, instead of marking them with unmeaning characters. And even if they were not practiced writers themselves, some secretary or scribe would have been called upon to act for them on such an occasion as this, if the art of writing had been at that time so generally known as to be customarily employed on public occasions. From these and similar indications which are found, on a careful examination, in the Homeric poems, learned men have concluded that they were composed and repeated orally, at a period of the world when the art of writing was very little known, and that they were handed down from generation to generation, through the memory of those who repeated them, until at last the art of writing became established among mankind, when they were at length put permanently upon record.

It seems that writing was not much employed for any of the ordinary and private purposes of life by the people of Greece until the article called papyrus was introduced among them. This took place about the year 600 before Christ, when laws began first to be written. Papyrus, like the art of writing upon it, came originally from Egypt. It was obtained from a tree which it seems grew only in that country. The tree flourished in the low lands along the margin of the Nile. It grew to the height of about ten feet. The paper obtained from it was formed from a sort of inner bark, which consisted of thin sheets or pellicles growing around the wood. The paper was manufactured in the following manner. A sheet of the thin bark was taken from the tree, was laid flat upon a board, and then a cross layer was laid over it, the materials having been previously moistened with water made slightly glutinous. The sheet thus formed was pressed and dried in the sun. The placing of two layers of the bark in this manner across each other was intended to strengthen the texture of the sheet, for the fibers, it was found, were very easily separated and torn so long as they lay wholly in one direction. The sheet when dry was finished by smoothing the surface, and prepared to receive inscriptions made by means of a pen fashioned from a reed or a quill.

In forming the papyrus into books it was customary to use a long sheet or web of it, and roll it upon a stick, as is the custom in respect to maps at the present day. The writing was in columns, each of which formed a sort of page, the reader holding the ends of the roll in his two hands, and reading at the part which was open between them. Of course, as he advanced, he continually unrolled on one side, and rolled up upon the other. Rolls of parchment were often made in the same manner.

The term volume used in respect to modern books, had its origin in this ancient practice of writing upon long rolls. The modern practice is certainly much to be preferred, though the ancient one was far less inconvenient than might at first be supposed. The long sheet was rolled upon a wooden billet, which gave to the volume a certain firmness and solidity, and afforded it great protection. The ends of this roller projected beyond the edges of the sheet, and were terminated in knobs or bosses, which guarded in some measure the edges of the papyrus or of the parchment. The whole volume was also inclosed in a parchment case, on the outside of which the title of the work was conspicuously recorded. Many of these ancient rolls have been found at Herculaneum.

For ink, various colored liquids were used, generally black, but sometimes red and sometimes green. The black ink was sometimes manufactured from a species of lampblack or ivory black, such as is often used in modern times for painting. Some specimens of the inkstands which were used in ancient times have been found at Herculaneum, and one of them contained ink, which though too thick to flow readily from the pen, it was still possible to write with. It was of about the consistency of oil.

These rolls of papyrus and parchment, however, were only used for important writings which it was intended permanently to preserve. For ordinary occasions tablets of wax and other similar materials were used, upon which the writer traced the characters with the point of a steel instrument called a style. The head of the style was smooth and rounded, so that any words which the writer wished to erase might be obliterated by smoothing over again, with it, the wax on which they had been written.

Such is a brief history of the rise and progress of the art of writing in the States of Greece. Whether the phonetic principle which Cadmus introduced was brought originally from Egypt, or from the countries on the eastern shore of the Mediterranean sea, can not now be ascertained. It has generally been supposed among mankind, at least until within a recent period, that the art of phonetic writing did not originate in Egypt, for the inscriptions on all the ancient monuments in that country are of such a character that it has always been supposed that they were symbolical characters altogether, and that no traces of any phonetic writing existed in that land. Within the present century, however, the discovery has been made that a large portion of these hieroglyphics are phonetic in their character; and that the learned world in attempting for so many centuries, in vain, to affix symbolical meanings to them, had been altogether upon the wrong track. The delineations, though they consist almost wholly of the forms of plants and animals, and of other natural and artificial objects, are not symbolical representations of ideas, but letters, representing sounds and words. They are thus precisely similar, in principle, to the letters of Cadmus, though wholly different from them in form.

To enable the reader to obtain a clearer idea of the nature of this discovery, we give on the adjoining page some specimens of Egyptian inscriptions found in various parts of the country, and which are interpreted to express the name Cleopatra, a very common name for princesses of the royal line in Egypt during the dynasty of the Ptolemy's. We mark the various figures forming the inscription, with the letters which modern interpreters have assigned to them. It will be seen that they all spell, rudely indeed, but yet tolerably distinctly, the name CLEOPATRA.

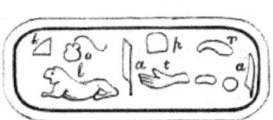

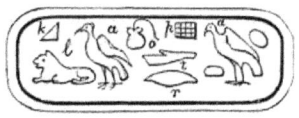

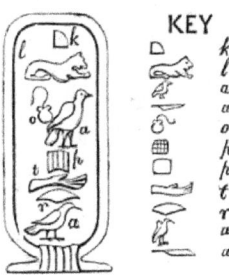

By a careful examination of these specimens, it will be seen that the order of placing the letters, if such hieroglyphical characters can be so called, is not regular, and the letter a, which is denoted by a bird in some of the specimens, is represented differently in others. There are also two characters at the close of each inscription which are not represented by any letter, the one being of the form of an egg, and the other a semicircle. These last are supposed to denote the sex of the sovereign whose name they are connected with, as they are found in many cases in inscriptions commemorative of princesses and queens. They are accordingly specimens of symbolic characters, while all the others in the name are phonetic.

It seems therefore not improbable that the principle of forming a written language by means of characters representing the sounds of which the words of the spoken language are composed, was of Egyptian origin; and that it was carried in very early times to the countries on the eastern shore of the Mediterranean sea, and there improved upon by the adoption of a class of characters more simple than the hieroglyphics of Egypt, and of a form more convenient for a regular linear arrangement in writing. Moses, who spent his early life in Egypt, and who was said to be learned in all the wisdom of the Egyptians, may have acquired the art of writing there.

However this may be, and whatever may be the uncertainty which hangs over the early history of this art, one thing is certain, and that is, that the discovery of the art of writing, including that of printing, which is only the consummation and perfection of it,—the art by which man can record language, and give life and power to the record to speak to the eye permanently and forever—to go to every nation—to address itself simultaneously to millions of minds, and to endure through all time, is by far the greatest discovery, in respect to the enlargement which it makes of human powers, that has ever been made.

3

The Story of Æneas

BESIDES the intrinsic interest and importance of the facts stated in the last chapter, to the student of history, there was a special reason for calling the attention of the reader to them here, that he might know in what light the story of the destruction of Troy, and of the wanderings of Æneas, the great ancestor of Romulus, which we now proceed to relate, is properly to be regarded. The events connected with the destruction of Troy, took place, if they ever occurred at all, about the year twelve hundred before Christ. Homer is supposed to have lived and composed his poems about the year nine hundred; and the art of writing is thought to have been first employed for the purpose of recording continuous compositions, about the year six hundred. The story of Æneas then, so far as it has any claims to historical truth, is a tale which was handed down by oral tradition, among story-tellers for three hundred years, and then was clothed in verse, and handed down in that form orally by the memory of the reciters of it, in generations successive for three hundred years more, before it was recorded; and during the whole period of this transmission, the interest felt in it was not the desire for ascertaining and communicating historic truth, but simply for entertaining companies of listeners with the details of a romantic story. The story, therefore, can not be relied upon as historically true; but it is no less important on that account, that all well-informed persons should know what it is.

The mother of Æneas (as the story goes), was a celebrated goddess. Her name was Aphrodite; though among the Romans she afterward received the name of Venus. Aphrodite was not born of a mother, like ordinary mortals, but sprang mysteriously and supernaturally from a foam which gathered on a certain occasion upon the surface of the sea. At the commencement of her existence she crept out upon the shores of an island that was near,—the island of Cythera,—which lies south of the Peloponnesus.

The Origin of Venus

She was the goddess of love, of beauty, and of fruitfulness; and so extraordinary were the magical powers which were inherent from the beginning, in her very nature, that as she walked along upon the sands of the shore, when she first emerged from the sea, plants and flowers of the richest verdure and beauty sprang up at her feet wherever she stepped. She was, besides, in her own person, inexpressibly beautiful; and in addition to the natural influence of her charms, she was endued with the supernatural power of inspiring the sentiment of love in all who beheld her.

From Cythera the goddess made her way over by sea to Cyprus, where she remained for some time, amid the gorgeous and magnificent scenery of that enchanting island. Here she had two children, beautiful boys. Their names were Eros and Anteros. Each of these children remained perpetually a child, and Eros, in later times called Cupid, became the god of "love bestowed," while Anteros was the God of "love returned." After this the mother and the boys roamed about the world,—now in the heavenly regions above, and now among mortals on the plains and in the valleys below: they sometimes appeared openly, in their true forms, sometimes they assumed disguises, and sometimes they were wholly invisible; but whether seen or unseen, they were always busy in performing their functions—the mother inspiring everywhere, in the minds both of gods and men, the tenderest sentiments of beauty and desire,—while Eros, awakened love in the heart of one person for another, and Anteros made it his duty to tease and punish those who thus became objects of affection, if they did not return the love.

After some time, Aphrodite and her boys found their way to the heavenly regions of Mount Olympus, where the great divinities resided, and there they soon produced great trouble, by enkindling the flames of love in the hearts of the divinities themselves, causing them, by her magic power, to fall in love not only with one another, but also with mortal men and women on the earth below. In retaliation upon Aphrodite for this mischief, Jupiter, by his supreme power, inspired Aphrodite herself with a sentiment of love. The object of her affection was Anchises, a handsome youth, of the royal family of Troy, who lived among the mountains of Ida, not far from the city.

The way in which it happened that the affection of Aphrodite turned toward an inhabitant of Mount Ida was this. There had been at one time a marriage among the divinities, and a certain goddess who had not been invited to the wedding, conceived the design of avenging herself for the neglect, by provoking a quarrel among those who were there. She, accordingly, caused a beautiful golden apple to be made, with an inscription marked upon it, "FOR THE MOST BEAUTIFUL." This apple she threw in among the guests assembled at the wedding. The goddesses all claimed the prize, and a very earnest dispute arose among them in respect to it. Jupiter sent the several claimants, under the charge of a special messenger, to Mount Ida, to a handsome and accomplished young shepherd there, named Paris—who was, in fact, a prince in disguise—that they might exhibit themselves to him, and submit the question of the right to the apple to his award. The contending goddesses appeared accordingly before Paris, and each attempted to bribe him to decide in her favor, by offering him some peculiar and tempting reward. Paris gave the apple to Aphrodite, and she was so pleased with the result, that she took Paris under her special protection, and made the solitudes of Mount Ida one of her favorite retreats.

Here she saw and became acquainted with Anchises, who was, as has already been said, a noble, or prince, by descent, though he had for some time been dwelling away from the city, and among the mountains, rearing flocks and herds. Here Aphrodite saw him, and when Jupiter inspired her with a sudden susceptibility to the power of love, the shepherd Anchises was the object toward which her affections turned. She accordingly went to Mount Ida, and giving herself up to him, she lived with him for some time among the mountains as his bride. Æneas was their son.

Aphrodite did not, however, appear to Anchises in her true character, but assumed, instead, the form and the disguise of a Phrygian princess. Phrygia was a kingdom of Asia Minor, not very far from Troy. She continued this disguise as long as she remained with Anchises at Mount Ida; at length, however, she concluded to leave him, and to return to Olympus, and at her parting she made herself known. She, however, charged Anchises never to reveal to any person who she was, declaring that Æneas, whom she was going to leave with his father when she went away, would be destroyed by a stroke of lightning from heaven, if the real truth in respect to his mother were ever revealed.

When Aphrodite had gone, Anchises, having now no longer any one at home to attend to the rearing of the child, sent him to Dardanus, a city to the northward of Troy, where he was brought up in the house of his sister the daughter of Anchises, who was married and settled there.

His having a sister old enough to be married, would seem to show that youth was not one of the attractions of Anchises in Aphrodite's eyes. Æneas remained with his sister until he was old enough to be of service in the care of flocks and herds, and then returned again to his former residence among the pasturages of the mountains. His mother, though she had left him, did not forget her child; but watched over him continually, and interposed directly to aid or to protect him, whenever her aid was required by the occurrence of any emergency of difficulty or danger.

At length the Trojan war broke out. For a time, however, Æneas took no part in it. He was jealous of the attentions which Priam, the king of Troy, paid to other young men, and fancied that he himself was overlooked and that the services that he might render were undervalued. He remained, therefore, at his home among the mountains, occupying himself with his flocks and herds; and he might, perhaps, have continued in these peaceful avocations to the end of the war, had it not been that Achilles, one of the most formidable of the Grecian leaders, in one of his forays in the country around Troy, in search of provisions, came upon Æneas's territory, and attacked him while tending his flocks upon the mountain side. Achilles seized the flocks and herds, and drove Æneas and his fellow-herdsmen away. They would, in fact, all have been killed, had not Aphrodite interposed to protect her son and save his life.

The loss of his flocks and herds, and the injury which he himself had received, aroused Æneas's indignation and anger against the Greeks. He immediately raised an armed force of Dardanians, and thenceforth took an active part in the war. He became one of the most distinguished among the combatants, for his prowess and his bravery; and being always assisted by his mother in his conflicts, and rescued by her when in danger, he performed prodigies of strength and valor.

At one time he pressed forward into the thickest of the battle to rescue a Trojan leader named Pandarus, who was beset by his foes and brought into very imminent danger. Æneas did not succeed in saving his friend. Pandarus was killed. Æneas, however, flew to the spot, and by means of the most extraordinary feats of strength and valor he drove the Greeks away from the body. They attacked it on every side, but Æneas, wheeling around it, and fighting now on this side and now on that, drove them all away. They retired to a little distance and then began to throw in a shower of spears and darts and arrows upon him. Æneas defended himself and the body of his friend from these missiles for a time, with his shield. At length, however, he was struck in the thigh with a ponderous stone which one of the Greek warriors hurled at him,—a stone so heavy that two men of ordinary strength would have been required to lift it. Æneas was felled to the ground by the blow. He sank down, resting upon his arm, faint and dizzy, and being thus made helpless would have immediately been overpowered and killed by his assailants had not his mother interposed. She came immediately to rescue him. She spread her vail over him, which had the magic power of rendering harmless all blows which were aimed at what was covered by it, and then taking him up in her arms she bore him off through the midst of his enemies unharmed. The swords, spears, and javelins which were aimed at him were rendered powerless by the magic vail.

Æneas Defending the Body of Pandarus

Aphrodite, however, flying thus with her wounded son, mother-like, left herself exposed in her anxiety to protect him. Diomedes, the chief of the pursuers, following headlong on, aimed a lance at Venus herself. The lance struck Venus in the hand, and inflicted a very severe and painful wound. It did not, however, stop her flight. She pressed swiftly on, while Diomedes, satisfied with his revenge, gave up the pursuit, but called out to Aphrodite as she disappeared from view, bidding her learn from the lesson which he had given her that it would be best for her thenceforth to remain in her own appropriate sphere, and not come down to the earth and interfere in the contests of mortal men.

Aphrodite, after conveying Æneas to a place of safety, fled, herself, faint and bleeding, to the mountains, where, after ascending to the region of mists and clouds, Iris, the beautiful goddess of the rainbow, came to her aid. Iris found her faint and pale from the loss of blood; she did all in her power to soothe and comfort the wounded goddess, and then led her farther still among the mountains to a place where they found Mars, the god of war, standing with his chariot. Mars was Aphrodite's brother. He took compassion upon his sister in her distress, and lent Iris his chariot and horses, to convey Aphrodite home. Aphrodite ascended into the chariot, and Iris took the reins; and thus they rode through the air to the mountains of Olympus. Here the gods and goddesses of heaven gathered around their unhappy sister, bound up her wound, and expressed great sympathy for her in her sufferings, uttering at the same time many piteous complaints against the merciless violence and inhumanity of men. Such is the ancient tale of Æneas and his mother.

At a later period in the history of the war, Æneas had a grand combat with Achilles, who was the most terrible of all the Grecian warriors, and was regarded as the grand champion of their cause. The two armies were drawn up in battle array. A vast open space was left between them on the open plain. Into this space the two combatants advanced, Æneas on the one side and Achilles on the other, in full view of all the troops, and of the throngs of spectators assembled to witness the proceedings.

A very strong and universal interest was felt in the approaching combat. Æneas, besides the prodigious strength and bravery for which he was renowned, was to be divinely aided, it was known, by the protection of his mother, who was always at hand to guide and support him in the conflict, and to succor him in danger. Achilles, on the other hand, possessed a charmed life. He had been dipped by his mother Thetis, when an infant, in the river Styx, to render him invulnerable and immortal; and the immersion produced the effect intended in respect to all those parts of the body which the water laved. As, however, Thetis held the child by the ankles when she plunged him in, the ankles remained unaffected by the magic influence of the water. All the other parts of the body were rendered incapable of receiving a wound.

Achilles had a very beautiful and costly shield which his mother had caused to be made for him. It was formed of five plates of metal. The outermost plates on each side were of brass; in the centre was a plate of gold; and between the central plate of gold and the outer ones of brass were two other plates, one on each side, made of some third metal. The workmanship of this shield was of the most elaborate and beautiful character. The mother of Achilles had given this weapon to her son when he left home to join the Greeks in the Trojan war, not trusting entirely it seems to his magical invulnerability.

The armies looked on with great interest as these two champions advanced to meet each other, while all the gods and goddesses surveyed the scene with almost equal interest, from their abodes above. Some joined Venus in the sympathy which she felt for her son, while others espoused the cause of Achilles. When the two combatants had approached each other, they paused before commencing the conflict, as is usual in such cases, and surveyed each other with looks of anger and defiance. At length Achilles spoke. He began to upbraid Æneas for his infatuation and folly in engaging in the war, and especially for coming forward to put his life at hazard by encountering such a champion as was now before him. "What can you gain," said he, "even if you conquer in this warfare? You can never be king, even if you succeed in saving the

ROMULUS: FOUNDER OF ROME

city. I know you claim to be descended from the royal line; but Priam has sons who are the direct and immediate heirs, and your claims can never be allowed. Then, besides, what folly to attempt to contend with me! Me, the strongest, bravest, and most terrible of the Greeks, and the special favorite of many deities." With this introduction Achilles went on to set forth the greatness of his pedigree, and the loftiness of his pretensions to superiority over all others in personal prowess and valor, in a manner very eloquent indeed, and in a style which it seems was very much admired in those days as evincing only a proper spirit and energy,—though in our times such a harangue would be very apt to be regarded as only a vainglorious and empty boasting.

Æneas replied,—retorting with vauntings on his side no less spirited and energetic than those which Achilles had expressed. He gave a long account of his pedigree, and of his various claims to lofty consideration. He, however, said, in conclusion, that it was idle and useless for them to waste their time in such a war of words, and so he hurled his spear at Achilles with all his force, as a token of the commencement of the battle.

The spear struck the shield of Achilles, and impinged upon it with such force that it penetrated through two of the plates of metal which composed the shield, and reached the central plate of gold, where the force with which it had been thrown being spent, it was arrested and fell to the ground. Achilles then exerting his utmost strength threw his spear in return. Æneas crouched down to avoid the shock of the weapon, holding his shield at the same time above his head, and bracing himself with all his force against the approaching concussion. The spear struck the shield near the upper edge of it, as it was held in Æneas's hands. It passed directly through the plates of which the shield was composed, and then continuing its course, it glided down just over Æneas's back, and planted itself deep in the ground behind him, and stood there quivering. Æneas crept out from beneath it with a look of horror.

Immediately after throwing his spear, and perceiving that it had failed of its intended effect, Achilles drew his sword and rushed forward to engage Æneas, hand to hand. Æneas himself recovering in an instant front the consternation which his narrow escape from impalement had awakened, seized an enormous stone, heavier, as Homer represents it, than any two ordinary men could lift, and was about to hurl it at his advancing foe, when suddenly the whole combat was terminated by a very unexpected interposition. It seems that the various gods and goddesses, from their celestial abodes among the summits of Olympus, had assembled in invisible forms to witness this combat—some sympathizing with and upholding one of the combatants, and some the other. Neptune was on Æneas's side; and accordingly when he saw how imminent the danger was which threatened Æneas, when Achilles came rushing upon him with his uplifted sword, he at once resolved to interfere. He immediately rushed, himself, between the combatants. He brought a sudden and supernatural mist over the scene, such as the God of the Sea has always at his command; and this mist at once concealed Æneas from Achilles's view. Neptune drew the spear out of the ground, and released it too from the shield which remained still pinned down by it; and then threw the spear down at Achilles's feet. He next seized Æneas, and lifting him high above the ground he bore him away in an invisible form over the heads of soldiers and horsemen that had been drawn up in long lines around the field of combat. When the mist passed away Achilles saw his spear lying at his feet, and on looking around him found that his enemy was gone.

Such are the marvelous tales which were told by the ancient narrators, of the prowess and exploits of Æneas under the walls of Troy, and of the interpositions which were put forth to save him in moments of desperate danger, by beings supernatural and divine. These tales were in those days believed as sober history. That which was marvelous and philosophically incredible in them, was sacredly sheltered from question by mingling itself with the prevailing principles of religious faith. The tales were thus believed, and handed down traditionally from generation to generation, and admired and loved by all who heard and repeated them, partly on account of their romantic and poetical beauty, and partly on account of the sublime and sacred revelations which they contained, in respect to the divinities of the spiritual world.

4

The Destruction of Troy

AFTER the final conquest and destruction of Troy, Æneas, in the course of his wanderings, stopped, it was said, at Carthage, on his way to Italy, and there, according to ancient story, he gave the following account of the circumstances attending the capture and the sacking of the city, and his own escape from the scene.

One day, after the war had been continued with various success for a long period of time, the sentinels on the walls and towers of the city began to observe extraordinary movements in the camp of the besiegers, which seemed to indicate preparations for breaking up the camp and going away. Tents were struck. Men were busy passing to and fro, arranging arms and military stores, as if for transportation. A fleet of ships was drawn up along the shore, which was not far distant, and a great scene of activity manifested itself upon the bank, indicating an approaching embarkation. In a word, the tidings soon spread throughout the city, that the Greeks had at length become weary of the protracted contest, and were making preparations to withdraw from the field. These proceedings were watched, of course, with great interest from the walls of the city, and at length the inhabitants, to their inexpressible joy, found their anticipations and hopes, as they thought, fully realized. The camp of the Greeks was gradually broken up, and at last entirely abandoned. The various bodies of troops were drawn off one by one to the shore, where they were embarked on board the ships, and then sailed away. As soon as this result was made sure, the Trojans threw open the gates of the city, and came out in throngs,—soldiers and citizens, men, women and children together,—to explore the abandoned encampment, and to rejoice over the departure of their terrible enemies.

The first thing which attracted their attention was an immense wooden horse, which stood upon the ground that the Greek encampment had occupied. The Trojans immediately gathered, one and all, around the monster, full of wonder and curiosity. Æneas, in narrating the story, says that the image was as large as a mountain; but, as he afterward relates that the people drew it on wheels within the walls of the city, and especially as he represents them as attaching the ropes for this purpose to the neck of the image, instead of to its fore-legs, which would have furnished the only proper points of attachment if the effigy had been of any very extraordinary size, he must have had a very small mountain in mind in making the comparison. Or, which is perhaps more probable, he used the term only in a vague metaphorical sense, as we do now when we speak of the waves of the ocean as running mountain high, when it is well ascertained that the crests of the billows, even in the most violent and most protracted storms, never rise more than twenty feet above the general level.

At all events, the image was large enough to excite the wonder of all the beholders. The Trojan people gathered around it, wholly unable to understand for what purpose the Greeks could have constructed such a monster, to leave behind them on their departure from Troy. After the first emotions of astonishment and wonder which the spectacle awakened, had somewhat subsided, there followed a consultation in respect to the disposal which was to be made of the prodigy. The opinions on this point were very various. One commander was disposed to consider the image a sacred prize, and recommended that they should convey it into the city, and deposit it in the citadel, as a trophy of victory. Another, dissenting decidedly from this counsel, said that he strongly suspected some latent treachery, and he proposed to build a fire under the body of the monster, and burn the image itself and all contrivances for mischief which might be contained in it, together. A third recommended that they should hew it open, and see for themselves what there might be within. One of the Trojan leaders named Laocoon, who, just at this juncture, came to the spot, remonstrated loudly and earnestly against having any thing to do with so mysterious and suspicious a prize, and, by way of expressing the strong animosity which he felt toward it, he hurled his spear with all his force against the monster's side. The spear stood trembling in the wood, producing a deep hollow sound by the concussion.

What the decision would have been in respect to the disposal of the horse, if this consultation and debate had gone on, it is impossible to say, as the farther consideration of the subject was all at once interrupted, by new occurrences which here suddenly intervened, and which, after engrossing for a time the whole attention of the company assembled, finally controlled the decision of the question. A crowd of peasants and shepherds were seen coming from the mountains, with much excitement, and loud shouts and outcries, bringing with them a captive Greek whom they had secured and bound. As the peasants came up with their prisoner, the Trojans gathered eagerly round them, full of excitement and threats of violence, all thirsting, apparently, for their victim's blood. He, on his part, filled the air with the most piteous lamentations and cries for mercy.

His distress and wretchedness, and the earnest entreaties which he uttered, seemed at length to soften the hearts of his enemies and finally, the violence of the crowd around the captive became somewhat appeased, and was succeeded by a disposition to question him, and hear what he had to say. The Greek told them, in answer to their interrogations, that his name was Sinon, and that he was a fugitive from his own countrymen the Greeks, who had been intending to kill him. He said that the Greek leaders had long been desirous of abandoning the siege of Troy, and that they had made many attempts to embark their troops and sail away, but that the winds and seas had risen against them on every such attempt, and defeated their design. They then sent to consult the oracle of Apollo, to learn what was the cause of the displeasure and hostility thus manifested against them by the god of the sea. The oracle replied, that they could not depart from Troy, till they had first made an atoning and propitiatory offering by the sacrifice of a man, such an one as Apollo himself might designate. When this answer was returned, the whole army, as Sinon said, was thrown into a state of consternation. No one knew but that the fatal designation might fall on him. The leaders were, however, earnestly determined on carrying the measure into effect. Ulysses called upon Calchas, the priest of Apollo, to point out the man who was to die. Calchas waited day after day, for ten days, before the divine intimation was made to him in respect to the individual who was to suffer. At length he said that Sinon was the destined victim. His comrades, Sinon said, rejoicing in their own escape from so terrible a doom, eagerly assented to the priest's decision, and immediately made preparations for the ceremony. The altar was reared. The victim was adorned for the sacrifice, and the garlands, according to the accustomed usage, were bound upon his temples. He contrived, however, he said, at the last moment, to make his escape. He broke the bands with which he had been bound, and fled into a morass near the shore, where he remained concealed in inaccessible thickets until the Greeks had sailed away. He then came forth and was at length seized and bound by the shepherds of the mountains, who found him wandering about, in extreme destitution and misery. Sinon concluded his tale by the most piteous lamentations, on his wretched lot. The Trojans, he supposed, would kill him, and the Greeks, on their return to his native land, in their anger against him for having made his escape from them, would destroy his wife and children.

The air and manner with which Sinon told this story seemed so sincere, and so natural and unaffected were the expressions of wretchedness and despair with which he ended his narrative, that the Trojan leaders had no suspicion that it was not true. Their compassion was moved for the wretched fugitive, and they determined to spare his life. Priam, the aged king, who was present at the scene, in the midst of the

Trojan generals, ordered the cords with which the peasants had bound the captive to be sundered, that he might stand before them free. The king spoke to him, too, in a kind and encouraging manner. "Forget your countrymen," said he. "They are gone. Henceforth you shall be one of us. We will take care of you." "And now," he continued, "tell us what this monstrous image means. Why did the Greeks make it, and why have they left it here?"

Sinon, as if grateful for the generosity with which his life had been spared, professed himself ready to give his benefactors the fullest information. He told them that the wooden horse had been built by the Greeks to replace a certain image of Pallas which they had previously taken and borne away from Troy. It was to replace this image, Sinon said, that the Greeks had built the wooden horse; and their purpose in making the image of this monstrous size was to prevent the possibility of the Trojans taking it into the city, and thus appropriating to themselves the benefit of its protecting efficacy and virtue.

The Trojans listened with breathless interest to all that Sinon said, and readily believed his story; so admirably well did he counterfeit, by his words and his demeanor, all the marks and tokens of honest sincerity in what he said of others, as well of grief and despair in respect to his own unhappy lot. The current of opinion which had begun before to set strongly in favor of destroying the horse, was wholly turned, and all began at once to look upon the colossal image as an object of sacred veneration, and to begin to form plans for transporting it within the limits of the city. Whatever remaining doubts any of them might have felt on the subject were dispelled by the occurrence of a most extraordinary phenomenon just at this stage of the affair, which was understood by all to be a divine judgment upon Laocoon for his sacrilegious temerity in striking his spear into the horse's side. It had been determined to offer a sacrifice to Neptune. Lots were drawn to determine who should perform the rite. The lot fell upon Laocoon. He began to make preparations to perform the duty, assisted by his two young sons, when suddenly two immense serpents appeared, coming up from the sea.

ROMULUS: FOUNDER OF ROME

They came swimming over the surface of the water, with their heads elevated above the waves, until they reached the shore, and then gliding swiftly along, they advanced across the plain, their bodies brilliantly spotted and glittering in the sun, their eyes flashing, and their forked and venomous tongues darting threats and defiance as they came. The people fled in dismay. The serpents, disregarding all others, made their way directly toward the affrighted children of Laocoon, and twining around them they soon held the writhing and struggling limbs of their shrieking victims hopelessly entangled in their deadly convolutions.

Laocoon, who was himself at a little distance from the spot, when the serpents came, as soon as he saw the danger and heard the agonizing cries of his boys, seized a weapon and ran to rescue them. Instead, however, of being able to save his children, he only involved himself in their dreadful fate. The serpents seized him as soon as he came within their reach, and taking two turns around his neck and two around his body, and binding in a remorseless gripe the forms of the fainting and dying boys with other convolutions, they raised their heads high above the group of victims which they thus enfolded, and hissed and darted out their forked tongues in token of defiance and victory. When at length their work was done, they glided away and took refuge in a temple that was near, and coiled themselves up for repose beneath the feet of the statue of a goddess that stood in the shrine.

The story of Laocoon has become celebrated among all mankind in modern times by means of a statue representing the catastrophe, which was found two or three centuries ago among the ruins of an ancient edifice at Rome. This statue was mentioned by an old Roman writer, Pliny, who gave an account of it while it yet stood in its place in the ancient city. He said that it was the work of three artists, a father and two sons, who combined their industry and skill to carve in one group, and with immense labor and care, the representation of Laocoon himself, the two boys, and the two serpents, making five living beings intertwined intricately together, and all carved from one single block of marble. On the decline and fall of Rome this statue was lost among the ruins of the city, and for many centuries it was known to mankind only through the description of Pliny. At length it was brought to light again, having been discovered about three centuries ago, under the ruins of the very edifice in which Pliny had described it as standing. It immediately became the object of great interest and attention to the whole world. It was deposited in the Vatican; a great reward was paid to the owner of the ground on which it was discovered; drawings and casts of it, without number, have been made; and the original stands in the Vatican now, an object of universal interest, as one of the most celebrated sculptures of ancient or modern times.

Laocoon himself forms the center of the group, with the serpents twined around him, while he struggles, with a fearful expression of terror and anguish in his countenance, in the vain attempt to release himself from their hold. One of the serpents has bitten one of the boys in the side, and the wounded child sinks under the effects of the poison. The other boy, in an agony of terror, is struggling, hopelessly, to release his foot from the convolutions with which one of the serpents has encircled it. The expression of the whole group is exciting and painful, and yet notwithstanding this, there is combined with it a certain mysterious grace and beauty which charms every eye, and makes the composition the wonder of mankind.

But to return to the story. The people understood this awful visitation to be the judgment of heaven against Laocoon for his sacrilegious presumption in daring to thrust his spear into the side of the image before them, and which they were now very sure they were to consider as something supernatural and divine. They determined with one accord to take it into the city.

They immediately began to make preparations for the transportation of it. They raised it from the ground, and fitted to the feet some sort of machinery of wheels or rollers, suitable to the nature of the ground, and strong enough to bear the weight of the colossal mass. They attached long ropes to the neck of the image, and extended them forward upon the ground and then brought up large companies of citizens and soldiers to man them. They arranged a procession, consisting of the generals of the army, and of the great civil dignitaries of the state; and in addition to these were groups of singing boys and girls, adorned with wreaths and garlands, who were appointed to chant sacred hymns to solemnize the occasion. They widened the access to the city, too, by tearing down a portion of the wall so as to open a sufficient space to enable the monster to get in. When all was ready the ropes were manned, the signal was given, the ponderous mass began to move, and though it encountered in its progress many difficulties, obstructions, and delays, in due time it was safely deposited in the court of a great public edifice within the city. The wall was then repaired, the day passed away, the night came on, the gates were shut, and the curiosity and wonder of the people within being gradually satisfied, they at length dispersed to their several homes and retired to rest. At midnight the unconscious effigy stood silent and alone where its worshipers had left it, while the whole population of the city were sunk in slumber, except the sentinels who had been stationed as usual to keep guard at the gates, or to watch upon the towers and battlements above them.

In the mean time the Greek fleet, which had sailed away under pretense of finally abandoning the country, had proceeded only to the island of Tenedos, which was about a league from the shore, and there they had concealed themselves during the day. As soon as night came on they returned to the main land, and disembarking with the utmost silence and secrecy, they made their way back again under cover of the darkness, as near as they dared to come to the gates of the city. In the mean time Sinon had arisen stealthily from the sleep which he had feigned to deceive those to whose charge he had been committed, and creeping cautiously through the streets he repaired to the place where the wooden horse had been deposited, and there opened a secret door in the side of the image, and liberated a band of armed and desperate men who had been concealed within. These men, as soon as they had descended to the ground and had adjusted their armor, rushed to the city walls, surprised and killed the sentinels and watchmen, threw open the gates, and gave the whole body of their comrades that were lurking outside the walls, in the silence and darkness of the night, an unobstructed admission.

Æneas was asleep in his house while these things were transpiring. The house where he lived was in a retired and quiet situation, but he was awakened from his sleep by distant outcries and din, and springing from his couch, and hastily resuming his dress, he ascended to the roof of the house to ascertain the cause of the alarm. He saw flames ascending from various edifices in the quarter of the city where the Greeks had come in. He listened. He could distinctly hear the shouts of men, and the notes of trumpets sounding the alarm. He immediately seized his armor and rushed forth into the streets, arousing the inhabitants around him from their slumbers by his shouts, and calling upon them to arm themselves and follow him.

In the midst of this excitement, there suddenly appeared before him, coming from the scene of the conflict, a Trojan friend, named Pantheus, who was hastening away from the danger, perfectly bewildered with excitement and agitation. He was leading with him his little son, who was likewise pale with terror. Æneas asked Pantheus what had happened. Pantheus in reply explained to him in hurried and broken words, that armed men, treacherously concealed within the wooden horse, had issued forth from their concealment, and had opened the gates of the city, and let the whole horde of their ferocious and desperate enemies in; that the sentinels and guards who had been stationed at the gates had been killed; and that the Greek troops had full possession of the city, and were barricading the streets and setting fire to the buildings on every side. "All is lost," said he, "our cause is ruined, and Troy is no more."

The announcing of these tidings filled Æneas and those who had joined him with a species of phrensy. They resolved to press forward into the combat, and there, if they must perish themselves, to carry down as many as possible of their enemies with them to destruction. They pressed on, therefore, through the gloomy streets, guiding their way toward the scene of action by the glare of the fires upon the sky, and by the sounds of the distant tumult and din.

They soon found themselves in the midst of scenes of dreadful terror and confusion,—the scenes, in fact, which are usually exhibited in the midnight sacking of a city. They met with various adventures during the time that they continued their desperate but hopeless resistance. They encountered a party of Greeks, and overpowered and slew them, and then, seizing the armor which their fallen enemies had worn, they disguised themselves in it, in hopes to deceive the main body of the Greeks by this means, so as to mingle among them unobserved, and thus attack and destroy such small parties as they might meet without being themselves attacked by the rest. They saw the princess Cassandra, the young daughter of king Priam, dragged away by Greek soldiers from a temple where she had sought refuge. They immediately undertook to rescue her, and were at once attacked both by the Greek party who had the princess in charge, and also by the Trojan soldiers, who shot arrows and darts down upon them from the roofs above, supposing, from the armor and the plumes which they wore, that they were enemies. They saw the royal palace besieged, and the tortoise formed for scaling the walls of it. The tumult and din, and the frightful glare of lurid flames by which the city was illuminated, formed a scene of inconceivable confusion and terror.

Æneas watched the progress of the assault upon the palace from the top of certain lofty roofs, to which he ascended for the purpose. Here there was a slender tower, which had been built for a watch-tower, and had been carried up to such a height that, from the summit of it, the watchmen stationed there could survey all the environs of the city, and on one side look off to some distance over the sea. This tower Æneas and the Trojans who were with him contrived to cut off at its base, and throw over upon the throngs of Grecians that were thundering at the palace gates below. Great numbers were killed by the falling ruins, and the tortoise was broken down. The Greeks, however, soon formed another tortoise, by means of which some of the soldiers scaled the walls, while others broke down the gates with battering rams and engines; and thus the palace, the sacred and last remaining stronghold of the city, was thrown open to the ferocious and frantic horde of its assailants.

The Falling Tower

The sacking of the palace presented an awful spectacle to the view of Æneas and his companions, as they looked down upon it from the roofs and battlements around. As the walls, one after another, fell in under the resistless blows dealt by the engines that were brought against them, the interior halls, and the most retired and private apartments, were thrown open to view—all illuminated by the glare of the surrounding conflagrations.

Shrieks and wailing, and every other species of outcry that comes from grief, terror, and despair, arose from within; and such spectators as had the heart to look continuously upon the spectacle, could see wretched men running to and fro, and virgins clinging to altars for protection, and frantic mothers vainly endeavoring to find hiding-places for themselves and their helpless children.

Priam the king, who was at this time old and infirm, was aroused from his slumbers by the dreadful din, and immediately began to seize his armor, and to prepare himself for rushing into the fight. His wife, however, Hecuba, begged and entreated him to desist. She saw that all was lost, and that any further attempts at resistance would only exasperate their enemies, and render their own destruction the more inevitable. She persuaded the king, therefore, to give up his weapons and go with her to an altar, in one of the courts of the palace,—a place which it would be sacrilege for their enemies to violate—and there patiently and submissively to await the end. Priam yielded to the queen's solicitations, and went with her to the place of refuge which she had chosen;—and the plan which they thus adopted, might very probably have been successful in saving their lives, had it not been for an unexpected occurrence which suddenly intervened, and which led to a fatal result. While they were seated by the altar, in attitudes of submission and suppliance, they were suddenly aroused by the rushing toward them of one of their sons, who came in, wounded and bleeding from some scene of combat, and pursued by angry and ferocious foes. The spent and fainting warrior sank down at the feet of his father and mother, and lay there dying and weltering in the blood which flowed from his wounds. The aged king was aroused to madness at this spectacle. He leaped to his feet, seized a javelin, and thundering out at the same time the most loud and bitter imprecations against the murderers of his son, he hurled the weapon toward them as they advanced. The javelin struck the shield of the leader of the assailants, and rebounded from it without producing any other effect than to enrage still more the furious spirit which it was meant to destroy. The assailant rushed forward, seized the aged father by the hair, dragged him slipping, as he went, in the blood of his son, up to the altar, and there plunged a sword into his body, burying it to the hilt,—and then threw him down, convulsed and dying, upon the body of his dying child.

Thus Priam fell, and with him the last hope of the people of Troy. The city in full possession of their enemies, the palace and citadel sacked and destroyed, and the king slain, they saw that there was nothing now left for which they had any wish to contend.

# 5

The Flight of Æneas

AENEAS, from his station upon the battlements of a neighboring edifice, witnessed the taking of the palace and the death of Priam. He immediately gave up all for lost, and turned his thoughts at once to the sole question of the means of saving himself and his family from impending destruction. He thought of his father, Anchises, who at this time lived with him in the city, and was nearly of the same age as Priam the king, whom he had just seen so cruelly slain. He thought of his wife too, whom he had left at home, and of his little son Ascanius, and he began now to be overwhelmed with the apprehension, that the besiegers had found their way to his dwelling, and were, perhaps, at that very moment plundering and destroying it and perpetrating cruel deeds of violence and outrage upon his wife and family. He determined immediately to hasten home.

He looked around to see who of his companions remained with him. There was not one. They had all gone and left him alone. Some had leaped down from the battlements and made their escape to other parts of the city. Some had fallen in the attempt to leap, and had perished in the flames that were burning among the buildings beneath them. Others still had been reached by darts and arrows from below, and had tumbled headlong from their lofty height into the street beneath them. The Greeks, too, had left that part of the city. When the destruction of the palace had been effected, there was no longer any motive to remain, and they had gone away, one band after another, with loud shouts of exultation and defiance, to seek new combats in other quarters of the city. Æneas listened to the sounds of their voices, as they gradually died away upon his ear. Thus, in one way and another, all had gone, and Æneas found himself alone.

Æneas contrived to find his way back safely to the street, and then stealthily choosing his way, and vigilantly watching against the dangers that surrounded him, he advanced cautiously among the ruins of the palace, in the direction toward his own home. He had not proceeded far before he saw a female figure lurking in the shadow of an altar near which he had to pass. It proved to be the princess Helen.

Helen

Helen was a Grecian princess, formerly the wife of Menelaus, king of Sparta, but she had eloped from Greece some years before, with Paris, the son of Priam, king of Troy, and this elopement had been the whole cause of the Trojan war. In the first instance, Menelaus, accompanied by another Grecian chieftain, went to Troy and demanded that Helen should be given up again to her proper husband. Paris refused to surrender her. Menelaus then returned to Greece and organized a grand expedition to proceed to Troy and recapture the queen. This was the origin of the war. The people, therefore, looked upon Helen as the cause, whether innocent or guilty, of all their calamities.

When Æneas, therefore, who was, as may well be supposed, in no very amiable or gentle temper, as he hurried along away from the smoking ruins of the palace toward his home, saw Helen endeavoring to screen herself from the destruction which she had been the means of bringing upon all that he held dear, he was aroused to a phrensy of anger against her, and determined to avenge the wrongs of his country by her destruction. "I will kill her," said he to himself, as he rushed forward toward the spot where she was concealed. "There is no great glory it is true in wreaking vengeance on a woman, or in bringing her to the punishment which her crimes deserve. Still I will kill her, and I shall be commended for the deed. She shall not, after bringing ruin upon us, escape herself, and go back to Greece in safety and be a queen there again."

Æneas said these words, rushing forward at the same time, sword in hand, he was suddenly intercepted and brought to a stand by the apparition of his mother, the goddess Aphrodite, who all at once stood in the way before him. She stopped him, took him by the hand, urged him to restrain his useless anger, and calmed and quieted him with soothing words. "It is not Helen," said she, "that has caused the destruction of Troy. It is through the irresistible and irrevocable decrees of the gods that the city has fallen. It is useless for you to struggle against inevitable destiny, or to attempt to take vengeance on mere human means and instrumentalities. Think no more of Helen. Think of your family. Your aged father, your helpless wife, your little son,—where are they? Even now while you are wasting time here in vain attempts to take vengeance on Helen for what the gods have done, all that are near and dear to you are surrounded by ferocious enemies thirsting for their blood. Fly to them and save them. I shall accompany you, though unseen, and will protect you and them from every impending danger."

As soon as Aphrodite had spoken these words she disappeared from view. Æneas, following her injunctions, went directly toward his home; and he found as he passed along the streets that the way was opened for him, by mysterious movements among the armed bands which were passing in every direction about the city, in such a manner as to convince him that his mother was really accompanying him, and protecting his way by her supernatural powers.

When he reached home the first person whom he saw was Anchises his father. He told Anchises that all was lost, and that nothing now remained for them but to seek safety for themselves by flying to the mountains behind the city. But Anchises refused to go. "You who are young," said he, "and who have enough of life before you to be worth preserving, may fly. As for me I will not attempt to save the little remnant that remains to me, to be spent, if saved, in miserable exile. If the powers of heaven had intended that I should have lived any longer, they would have spared my native city,—my only home. You may go yourselves, but leave me here to die."

In saying these words Anchises turned away in great despondency, firmly fixed, apparently, in his determination to remain and share the fate of the city. Æneas and Creusa his wife joined their entreaties in urging him to go away. But he would not be persuaded. Æneas then declared that he would not go and leave his father. If one was to die they would all die, he said, together. He called for his armor and began to put it on, resolving to go out again into the streets of the city and die, since he must die, in the act of destroying his destroyers.

He was, however, prevented from carrying this determination into effect, by Creusa's intervention, who fell down before him at the threshold of the door, almost frantic with excitement and terror, and holding her little son Ascanius with one arm, and clasping her husband's knees with the other, she begged him not to leave them. "Stay and save us," said she; "do not go and throw your life away. Or, if you will go, take us with you that we may all die together."

The conflict of impulses and passions in this unhappy family continued for some time longer, but it ended at last in the yielding of Anchises to the wishes of the rest, and they all resolved to fly. In the mean time, the noise and uproar in the streets of the city, were drawing nearer and nearer, and the light of the burning buildings breaking out continually at new points in the progress of the conflagration, indicated that no time was to be lost. Æneas hastily formed his plan. His father was too old and infirm to go himself through the city. Æneas determined therefore to carry him upon his shoulders. Little Ascanius was to walk along by his side. Creusa was to follow, keeping as close as possible to her husband lest she should lose him in the darkness of the night, or in the scenes of uproar and confusion through which they would have to pass on the way. The domestics of the family were to escape from the city by different routes, each choosing his own, in order to avoid attracting the attention of their enemies; and when once without the gates they were all to rendezvous again at a certain rising ground, not far from the city, which Æneas designated to them by means of an old deserted temple which marked the spot, and a venerable cypress which grew there.

This plan being formed the party immediately proceeded to put it in execution. Æneas spread a lion's skin over his shoulders to make the resting-place more easy for his father, or perhaps to lighten the pressure of the heavy burden upon his own limbs. Anchises took what were called the household gods, in his hands. These were sacred images which it was customary to keep, in those days, in every dwelling, as the symbol and embodiment of divine protection. To save these images, when every thing else was given up for lost, was always the object of the last desperate effort of the husband and father. Æneas in this case asked his father to take these images, as it would have been an impiety for him, having come fresh from scenes of battle and bloodshed, to have put his hand upon them, without previously performing some ceremony of purification. Ascanius took hold of his father's hand. Creusa followed behind. Thus arranged they sallied forth from the house into the streets—all dark and gloomy, except so far as they received a partial and inconstant light from the flames of the distant conflagrations, which glared in the sky, and flashed sometimes upon battlements and towers, and upon the tops of lofty dwellings.

Æneas pressed steadily on, though in a state continually of the highest excitement and apprehension. He kept stealthily along wherever he could find the deepest shadows, under walls, and through the most obscure and the narrowest streets. He was in constant fear lest some stray dart or arrow should strike Anchises or Creusa, or lest some band of Greeks should come suddenly upon them, in which case he knew well that they would all be cut down without mercy, for, loaded down as he was with his burden, he would be entirely unable to do any thing to defend either himself or them. The party, however, for a time seemed to escape all these dangers, but at length, just as they were approaching the gate of the city, and began to think that they were safe, they were suddenly alarmed by a loud uproar, and by a rush of men which came in toward them from some streets in that quarter of the city, and threatened to overwhelm them. Anchises was greatly alarmed. He saw the gleaming weapons of the Greeks who were rushing toward them, and he called out to Æneas to fly faster, or to turn off some other way, in order to escape the impending danger. Æneas was terrified by the shouts and uproar which he heard, and his mind was for a moment confused by the bewildering influences of the scene. He however hurried forward, running this way and that, wherever there seemed the best prospect of escape, and often embarrassed and retarded in his flight by the crowds of people who were moving confusedly in all directions. At length, however, he succeeded in finding egress from the city. He pressed on, without stopping to look behind him till he reached the appointed place of rendezvous on the hill, and then gently laying down his burden, he looked around for Creusa. She was nowhere to be seen.

Æneas was in utter consternation, at finding that his wife was gone. He mourned and lamented this dreadful calamity with loud exclamations of grief and despair; then reflecting that it was a time for action and not for idle grief, he hastened to conceal his father and Ascanius in a dark and winding valley behind the hill, and leaving them there under the charge of his domestics, he hastened back to the city to see if Creusa could be found.

He armed himself completely before he went, being in his desperation determined to encounter every danger in his attempts to find and to recover his beloved wife. He went directly to the gate from which he had come out, and re-entering the city there, he began to retrace, as well as he could, the way that he had taken in coming out of the city— guiding himself as he went, by the light of the flames which rose up here and there from the burning buildings.

He went on in this way in a desperate state of agitation and distress, searching everywhere but seeing nothing of Creusa. At length he thought it possible that she had concluded, when she found herself separated from him, to go back to the house, as the safest place of refuge for her, and he determined, accordingly, to go and seek her there. This was his last hope, and most cruelly was it disappointed when he came to the place of his dwelling.

He found his house, when he arrived near the spot, all in flames. The surrounding buildings were burning too, and the streets in the neighborhood were piled up with furniture and goods which the wretched inmates of the dwellings had vainly endeavored to save. These inmates themselves were standing around, distracted with grief and terror, and gazing hopelessly upon the scene of devastation before them.

Æneas saw all these things at a glance, and immediately, in a frenzy of excitement, began to call out Creusa's name. He went to and fro among the groups surrounding the fire, calling for her in a frantic manner, and imploring all whom he saw to give him some tidings of her. All was, however, in vain. She could not be found. Æneas then went roaming about through other portions of the city, seeking her everywhere, and inquiring for her of every person whom he met that had the appearance of being a friend. His suspense, however, was terminated at last by his suddenly coming upon an apparition of the spirit of Creusa, which rose before him in a solitary part of the city, and arrested his progress. The apparition was of preternatural size, and it stood before him in so ethereal and shadow-like a form, and the features beamed upon him with so calm and placid and benignant an expression, as convinced him that the vision was not of this world. Æneas saw at a glance that Creusa's earthly sorrows and sufferings were ended forever.

At first he was shocked and terrified at the spectacle. Creusa, however, endeavored to calm and quiet him by soothing words. "My dearest husband," said she, "do not give way thus to anxiety and grief. The events which have befallen us, have not come by chance. They are all ordered by an overruling providence that is omnipotent and divine. It was predetermined by the decrees of heaven that you were not to take me with you in your flight. I have learned what your future destiny is to be. There is a long period of weary wandering before you, over the ocean and on the land, and you will have many difficulties, dangers, and trials to incur. You will, however, be conducted safely through them all, and will in the end find a peaceful and happy home on the banks of the Tiber. There you will found a new kingdom; a princess is even now provided for you there, to become your bride. Cease then to mourn for me; rather rejoice that I did not fall a captive into the hands of our enemies, to be carried away into Greece and made a slave. I am free, and you must not lament my fate. Farewell. Love Ascanius for my sake, and watch over him and protect him as long as you live."

Having spoken these words, the vision began to disappear. Æneas endeavored to clasp the beloved image in his arms to retain it, but it was intangible and evanescent, and, before he could speak to it, it was gone, and he was left standing in the desolate and gloomy street alone. He turned at length slowly away; and solitary, thoughtful and sad, he went back to the gate of the city, and thence out to the valley where he had concealed Anchises and his little son.

He found them safe. The whole party then sought places of retreat among the glens and mountains, where they could remain concealed a few days, while Æneas and his companions could make arrangements for abandoning the country altogether. These arrangements were soon completed. As soon as the Greeks had retired, so that they could come out without danger from their place of retreat, Æneas employed his men in building a number of small vessels, fitting them, as was usual in those days, both with sails and oars.

During the progress of these preparations, small parties of Trojans were coming in continually, day by day, to join him; being drawn successively from their hiding-places among the mountains, by hearing that the Greeks had gone away, and that Æneas was gradually assembling the remnant of the Trojans on the shore. The numbers thus collected at Æneas's encampment gradually increased, and as Æneas enlarged and extended his naval preparations to correspond with the augmenting numbers of his adherents, he found when he was ready to set sail, that he was at the head of a very respectable naval and military force.

When the fleet at last was ready, he put a stock of provisions on board, and embarked his men,—taking, of course, Anchises and Ascanius with him. As soon as a favorable wind arose, the expedition set sail. As the vessels moved slowly away, the decks were covered with men and women, who gazed mournfully at the receding shores, conscious that they were bidding a final farewell to their native land.

The nearest country within reach in leaving the Trojan coast, was Thrace—a country lying north of the Ægean Sea, and of the Propontis, being separated, in fact, in one part, from the Trojan territories, only by the Hellespont. Æneas turned his course northward toward this country, and, after a short voyage, landed there, and attempted to make a settlement. He was, however, prevented from remaining long, by a dreadful prodigy which he witnessed there, and which induced him to leave those shores very precipitously. The prodigy was this:

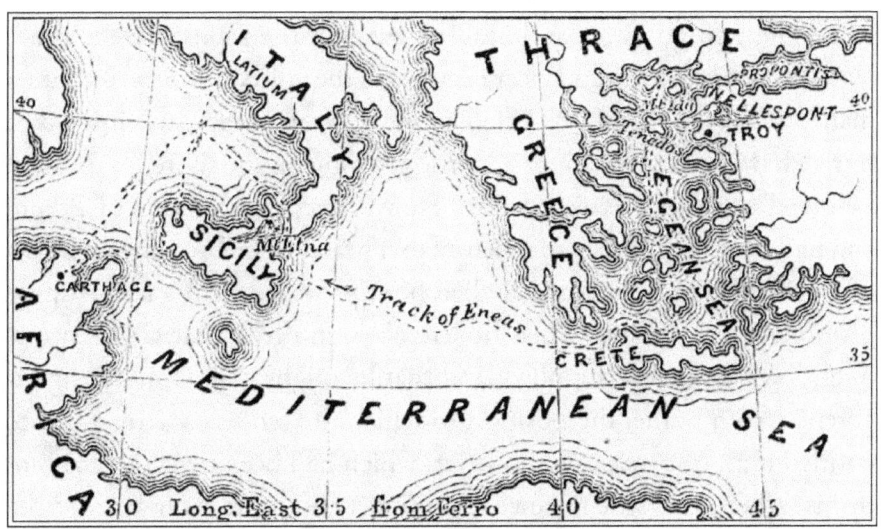

The Wanderings of Æneas

They had erected an altar on the shore, after they had landed, and were preparing to offer the sacrifices customary on such occasions, when Æneas, wishing to shade the altar with boughs, went to a myrtle bush which was growing near, and began to pull up the green shoots from the ground. To his astonishment and horror, he found that blood flowed from the roots whenever they were broken. Drops of what appeared to be human blood would ooze from the ruptured part as he held the shoot in his hand, and fall slowly to the ground. He was greatly terrified at this spectacle, considering it as some omen of very dreadful import. He immediately and instinctively offered up a prayer to the presiding deities of the land, that they would avert from him the evil influences, whatever they might be, which the omen seemed to portend, or that they would at least explain the meaning of the prodigy. After offering this prayer, he took hold of another stem of the myrtle, and attempted to draw it from the ground, in order to see whether any change in the appearances exhibited by the prodigy had been effected by his prayer. At the instant, however, when the roots began to give way, he heard a groan coming up from the ground below, as if from a person in suffering. Immediately afterward a voice, in a mournful and sepulchral accent, began to beg him to go away, and cease disturbing the repose of the dead. "What you are tearing and lacerating," said the voice, "is not a tree, but a man. I am Polydorus. I was killed by the king of Thrace, and instead of burial, have been turned into a myrtle growing on the shore."

Polydorus was a Trojan prince. He was the youngest son of Priam, and had been sent some years before to Thrace, to be brought up in the court of the Thracian king. He had been provided with a large supply of money and treasure when he left Troy, in order that all his wants might be abundantly supplied, and that he might maintain, during his absence from home, the position to which the rank as a Trojan prince entitled him. His treasures, however, which had been provided for him by his father as his sure reliance for support and protection, became the occasion of his ruin—for the Thracian king, when he found that the war was going against the Trojans, and that Priam the father was slain, and the city destroyed, murdered the helpless son to get possession of his gold.

Æneas and his companions were shocked to hear this story, and perceived at once that Thrace was no place of safety for them. They resolved immediately to leave the coast and seek their fortunes in other regions. They however, first, in secrecy and silence, but with great solemnity, performed those funeral rites for Polydorus which were considered in those ages essential to the repose of the dead. When these mournful ceremonies were ended they embarked on board their ships again and sailed away.

After this, the party of Æneas spent many months in weary voyages from island to island, and from shore to shore, along the Mediterranean sea, encountering every imaginable difficulty and danger, and meeting continually with the strangest and most romantic adventures. At one time they were misled by a mistaken interpretation of prophecy to attempt a settlement in Crete—a green and beautiful island lying south of the Ægean sea. They had applied to a sacred oracle, which had its seat at a certain consecrated spot which they visited in the course of their progress southward through the Ægean sea, asking the oracle to direct them where to go in order to find a settled home. The oracle, in answer to their request, informed them that they were to go to the land that their ancestors had originally come from, before their settlement in Troy. Æneas applied to Anchises to inform them what land this was. Anchises replied, that he thought it was Crete. There was an ancient tradition, he said, that some distinguished men among the ancestors of the Trojans had originated in Crete; and he presumed accordingly that that was the land to which the oracle referred.

The course of the little fleet was accordingly directed southward, and in due time the expedition safely reached the island of Crete, and landed there. They immediately commenced the work of effecting a settlement. They drew the ships up upon the shore; they laid out a city; they inclosed and planted fields, and began to build their houses. In a short time, however, all their bright prospects of rest and security were blighted by the breaking out of a dreadful pestilence among them. Many died; others who still lived, were utterly prostrated by the effects of the disease, and crawled about, emaciated and wretched, a miserable and piteous spectacle to behold. To crown their misfortunes, a great drought came on. The grain which they had planted was dried up and killed in the fields; and thus, in addition to the horrors of pestilence, they were threatened with the still greater horrors of famine. Their distress was extreme, and they were utterly at a loss to know what to do.

In this extremity Anchises recommended that they should send back to the oracle to inquire more particularly in respect to the meaning of the former response, in order to ascertain whether they had, by possibility, misinterpreted it, and made their settlement on the wrong ground. Or, if this was not the case, to learn by what other error or fault they had displeased the celestial powers, and brought upon themselves such terrible judgments. Æneas determined to adopt this advice, but he was prevented from carrying his intentions into effect by the following occurrence.

One night he was lying upon his couch in his dwelling,—so harassed by his anxieties and cares that he could not sleep, and revolving in his mind all possible plans for extricating himself and his followers from the difficulties which environed them. The moon shone in at the windows, and by the light of this luminary he saw, reposing in their shrines in the opposite side of the apartment where he was sleeping, the household images which he had rescued from the flames of Troy. As he looked upon these divinities in the still and solemn hour of midnight, oppressed with anxiety and care, one of them began to address him.

"We are commissioned," said this supernatural voice, "by Apollo, whose oracle you are intending to consult again, to give you the answer that you desire, without requiring you to go back to his temple. It is true that you have erred in attempting to make a settlement in Crete. This is not the land which is destined to be your home. You must leave these shores, and continue your voyage. The land which is destined to receive you is Italy, a land far removed from this spot, and your way to it lies over wide and boisterous seas. Do not be discouraged, however, on this account, or on account of the calamities which now impend over you. You will be prospered in the end. You will reach Italy in safety, and there you will lay the foundations of a mighty empire, which in days to come will extend its dominion far and wide among the nations of the earth. Take courage, then, and embark once more in your ships with a cheerful and confident heart. You are safe, and in the end all will turn out well."

The strength and spirits of the desponding adventurer were very essentially revived by this encouragement. He immediately prepared to obey the injunctions which had been thus divinely communicated to him, and in a short time the half-built city was abandoned, and the expedition once more embarked on board the fleet and proceeded to sea. They met in their subsequent wanderings with a great variety of adventures, but it would extend this portion of our narrative too far, to relate them all. They encountered a storm by which for three days and three nights they were tossed to and fro, without seeing sun or stars, and of course without any guidance whatever; and during all this time they were in the most imminent danger of being overwhelmed and destroyed by the billows which rolled sublimely and frightfully around them. At another time, having landed for rest and refreshment among a group of Grecian islands, they were attacked by the harpies, birds of prey of prodigious size and most offensive habits, and fierce and voracious beyond description. The harpies were celebrated, in fact, in many of the ancient tales, as a race of beings that infested certain shores, and often teased and tormented the mariners and adventurers that happened to come among them. Some said, however, that there was not a race of such beings, but only two or three in all, and they gave their names. And yet different narrators gave different names, among which were Aëlopos, Nicothoë, Ocythoë, Ocypoæ, Celæno, Acholoë, and Aëllo. Some said that the harpies had the faces and forms of women. Others described them as frightfully ugly; but all agree in representing them as voracious beyond description, always greedily devouring every thing that they could get within reach of their claws.

These fierce monsters flew down upon Æneas and his party, and carried away the food from off the table before them; and even attacked the men themselves. The men then armed themselves with swords, secretly, and waited for the next approach of the harpies, intending to kill them, when they came near. But the nimble marauders eluded all their blows, and escaped with their plunder as before. At length the expedition was driven away from the island altogether, by these ravenous fowls, and when they were embarking on board of their vessels, the leader of the harpies perched herself upon a rock overlooking the scene, and in a human voice loaded Æneas and his companions, as they went away, with taunts and execrations.

The expedition passed one night in great terror and dread in the vicinity of Mount Etna, where they had landed. The awful eruptions of smoke, and flame, and burning lava, which issued at midnight from the summit of the mountain,—the thundering sounds which they heard rolling beneath them, through the ground, and the dread which was inspired in their minds by the terrible monsters that dwelt beneath the mountains, as they supposed, and fed the fires, all combined to impress them with a sense of unutterable awe; and as soon as the light of the morning enabled them to resume their course, they made all haste to get away from so appalling a scene. At another time they touched upon a coast which was inhabited by a race of one-eyed giants,—monsters of enormous magnitude and of remorseless cruelty. They were cannibals, —feeding on the bodies of men whom they killed by grasping them in their hands and beating them against the rocks which formed the sides of their den. Some men whom one of these monsters, named Polyphemus, had shut up in his cavern, contrived to surprise their keeper in his sleep, and though they were wholly unable to kill him on account of his colossal magnitude, they succeeded in putting out his eye, and Æneas and his companions saw the blinded giant, as they passed along the coast, wading in the sea, and bathing his wound. He was guiding his footsteps as he walked, by means of the trunk of a tall pine which served him for a staff.

At length, however, after the lapse of a long period of time, and after meeting with a great variety of adventures to which we can not even here allude, Æneas and his party reached the shores of Italy, at the point which by divine intimations had been pointed out to them as the place where they were to land.

The story of the life and adventures of Æneas, which we have given in this and in the preceding chapters, is a faithful summary of the narrative which the poetic historians of those days recorded. It is, of course, not to be relied upon as a narrative of facts; but it is worthy of very special attention by every cultivated mind of the present day, from the fact, that such is the beauty, the grace, the melody, the inimitable poetic perfection with which the story is told, in the language in which the original record stands, that the narrative has made a more deep and widespread, and lasting impression upon the human mind than any other narrative perhaps that ever was penned.

6

The Landing in Latium

LATIUM was the name given to an ancient province of Italy, lying south of the Tiber. At the time of Æneas's arrival upon the coast it was an independent kingdom. The name of the king who reigned over it at this period was Latinus.

The country on the banks of the Tiber, where the city of Rome afterward arose, was then a wild but picturesque rural region, consisting of hills and valleys, occupied by shepherds and husbandmen, but with nothing upon it whatever, to mark it as the site of a city. The people that dwelt in Latium were shepherds and herdsmen, though there was a considerable band of warriors under the command of the king. The inhabitants of the country were of Greek origin, and they had brought with them from Greece, when they colonized the country, such rude arts as were then known. They had the use of Cadmus's letters, for writing, so far as writing was employed at all in those early days. They were skillful in making such weapons of war, and such simple instruments of music, as were known at the time, and they could erect buildings, of wood, or of stone, and thus constructed such dwellings as they needed, in their towns, and walls and citadels for defence.

Æneas brought his fleet into the mouth of the Tiber, and anchored it there. He himself, and all his followers were thoroughly weary of their wanderings, and hoped that they were now about to land where they should find a permanent abode. The number of ships and men that had formed the expedition at the commencement of the voyage, was very large; but it had been considerably diminished by the various misfortunes and accidents incident to such an enterprise, and the remnant that was left longed ardently for rest. Some of the ships took fire, and were burned at their moorings in the Tiber, immediately after the arrival of the expedition. It was said that they were set on fire by the wives and mothers belonging to the expedition,—who wished, by destroying the ships, to render it impossible for the fleet to go to sea again.

However this may be, Æneas was very strongly disposed to make the beautiful region which he now saw before him, his final home. The country, in every aspect of it, was alluring in the highest degree. Level plains, varied here and there by gentle elevations, extended around him, all adorned with groves and flowers, and exhibiting a luxuriance in the verdure of the grass and in the foliage of the trees that was perfectly enchanting to the sea-weary eyes of his company of mariners. In the distance, blue and beautiful mountains bounded the horizon, and a soft, warm summer haze floated over the whole scene, bathing the landscape in a rich mellow light peculiar to Italian skies.

As soon as the disembarkation was effected, lines of encampment were marked out, at a suitable place on the shore, and such simple fortifications as were necessary for defence in such a case, were thrown up. Æneas dispatched one party in boats to explore the various passages and channels which formed the mouth of the river, perhaps in order to be prepared to make good his escape again, to sea, in case of any sudden or extraordinary danger. Another party were employed in erecting altars, and preparing for sacrifices and other religious celebrations, designed on the part of Æneas to propitiate the deities of the place, and to inspire his men with religious confidence and trust. He also immediately proceeded to organize a party of reconnoiterers who were to proceed into the interior, to explore the country and to communicate with the inhabitants.

Map of Latium

The party of reconnoiterers thus sent out followed up the banks of the river, and made excursions in various directions across the fields and plains. They found that the country was everywhere verdant and beautiful, and that it was covered in the interior with scattered hamlets and towns. They learned the name of the king, and also that of the city which he made his capitol. Latinus himself at the same time, heard the tidings of the arrival of these strangers. His first impulse was immediately to make an onset upon them with all his forces, and drive them away from his shores. On farther inquiry, however, he learned that they were in a distressed and suffering condition, and from the descriptions which were given him of their dress and demeanor he concluded that they were Greeks. This idea awakened in his mind some apprehension;

for the Greeks were then well known throughout the world, and were regarded everywhere as terrible enemies. Besides his fears, his pity and compassion were awakened, too, in some degree; and he was on the whole for a time quite at a loss to know what course to pursue in respect to the intruders.

In the mean time Æneas concluded to send an embassy to Latinus to explain the circumstances under which he had been induced to land so large a party on the Italian coast. He accordingly designated a considerable number of men to form this embassy, and giving to some of the number his instructions as to what they were to say to Latinus, he committed to the hands of the others a large number of gifts which they were to carry and present to him. These gifts consisted of weapons elaborately finished, vessels of gold or silver, embroidered garments, and such other articles as were customarily employed in those days as propitiatory offerings in such emergencies. The embassy when all was arranged proceeded to the Latian capital.

When they came in sight of it they found that it was a spacious city, with walls around it, and turrets and battlements within, rising here and there above the roofs of the dwellings. Outside the gates a portion of the population were assembled busily engaged in games, and in various gymnastic and equestrian performances. Some were driving furiously in chariots around great circles marked out for the course. Others were practicing feats of horsemanship, or running races upon fleet chargers. Others still were practicing with darts, or bows and arrows, or javelins; either to test and improve their individual skill, or else to compete with each other for victory or for a prize. The embassadors paused when they came in view of this scene, and waited until intelligence could be sent in to the monarch, informing him of their arrival.

Latinus decided immediately to admit the embassy to an audience, and they were accordingly conducted into the city. They were led, after entering by the gates, through various streets, until they came at length to a large public edifice, which seemed to be, at the same time, palace, senate-house, and citadel. There were to be seen, in the avenues which led to this edifice, statues of old warriors, and various other martial decorations. There were many old trophies of former victories preserved here, such as arms, and chariots, and prows of ships, and crests, and great bolts and bars taken from the gates of conquered cities,—all old, war-worn, and now useless, but preserved as memorials of bravery and conquest. The Trojan embassy, passing through and among these trophies, as they stood or hung in the halls and vestibules of the palace, were at length ushered into the presence of Latinus the king.

Here, after the usual ceremonies of introduction were performed, they delivered the message which Æneas had intrusted to them. They declared that they had not landed on Latinus's shore with any hostile intent. They had been driven away, they said, from their own homes, by a series of dire calamities, which had ended, at last, in the total destruction of their native city. Since then they had been driven to and fro at the mercy of the winds and waves, exposed to every conceivable degree of hardship and danger. Their landing finally in the dominions of Latinus in Italy, was not, they confessed, wholly undesigned, for Latium had been divinely indicated to them, on their way, as the place destined by the decrees of heaven for their final home. Following these indications, they had sought the shores of Italy and the mouths of the Tiber, and having succeeded in reaching them, had landed; and now Æneas, their commander, desired of the king that he would allow them to settle in his land in peace, and that he would set apart a portion of his territory for them, and give them leave to build a city.

The effect produced upon the mind of Latinus by the appearance of these embassadors, and by the communication which they made to him, proved to be highly favorable. He received the presents, too, which they had brought him, in a very gracious manner, and appeared to be much pleased with them. He had heard, as would seem, rumors of the destruction of Troy, and of the departure of Æneas's squadron; for a long time had been consumed by the wanderings of the expedition along the Mediterranean shores, so that some years had now elapsed since the destruction of Troy and the first sailing of the fleet. In a word,

Latinus soon determined to accede to the proposals of his visitors, and he concluded with Æneas a treaty of alliance and friendship. He designated a spot where the new city might be built, and all things were thus amicably settled.

There was one circumstance which exerted a powerful influence in promoting the establishment of friendly relations between Latinus and the Trojans, and that was, that Latinus was engaged, at the time of Æneas's arrival, in a war with the Rutulians, a nation that inhabited a country lying south of Latium and on the coast. Latinus thought that by making the Trojans his friends, he should be able to enlist them as his auxiliaries in this war. Æneas made no objection to this, and it was accordingly agreed that the Trojans, in return for being received as friends, and allowed to settle in Latium, were to join with their protectors in defending the country, and were especially to aid them in prosecuting the existing war.

In a short time a still closer alliance was formed between Æneas and Latinus, an alliance which in the end resulted in the accession of Æneas to the throne of Latinus. Latinus had a daughter named Lavinia. She was an only child, and was a princess of extraordinary merit and beauty. The name of the queen, her mother, the wife of Latinus, was Amata. Amata had intended her daughter to be the wife of Turnus, a young prince of great character and promise, who had been brought up in Latinus's court. Turnus was, in fact, a distant relative of Amata, and the plan of the queen was that he should marry Lavinia, and in the end succeed with her, to the throne of Latinus. Latinus himself had not entered into this scheme; and when closing his negotiations with Æneas, it seemed to him that it would be well to seal and secure the adherence of Æneas to his cause by offering him his daughter Lavinia for his bride. Æneas was very willing to accede to this proposal. What the wishes of Lavinia herself were in respect to the arrangement, it is not very well known; nor were her wishes, according to the ideas that prevailed in those times, of any consequence whatever. The plan was arranged, and the nuptials were soon to be celebrated. Turnus, when he found that he was to be superseded, left the court of Latinus, and went away out of the country in a rage.

Æneas and his followers seemed now to have come to the end of all their troubles. They were at last happily established in a fruitful land, surrounded by powerful friends, and about to enter apparently upon a long career of peaceful and prosperous industry. They immediately engaged with great ardor in the work of building their town. Æneas had intended to have named it Troy, in commemoration of the ancient city now no more. But, in view of his approaching marriage with Lavinia, he determined to change this design, and, in honor of her, to name the new capital Lavinium.

The territory which had been assigned to the Trojans by Latinus was in the south-western part of Latium, near the coast, and of course it was on the confines of the country of the Rutulians. Turnus, when he left Latium, went over to the Rutulians, determining, in his resentment against Latinus for having given Lavinia to his rival, to join them in the war. The Rutulians made him their leader, and he soon advanced at the head of a great army across the frontier, toward the new city of Lavinium. Thus Æneas found himself threatened with a very formidable danger.

Nor was this all. For just before the commencement of the war with Turnus, an extraordinary train of circumstances occurred which resulted in alienating the Latins themselves from their new ally, and in leaving Æneas consequently to sustain the shock of the contest with Turnus and his Rutulians alone. It would naturally be supposed that the alliance between Latinus and Æneas would not be very favorably regarded by the common people of Latium. They would, on the other hand, naturally look with much jealousy and distrust on a company of foreign intruders, admitted by what they would be very likely to consider the capricious partiality of their king, to a share of their country. This jealousy and distrust was, for a time, suppressed and concealed; but the animosity only acquired strength and concentration by being restrained, and at length an event occurred which caused it to break forth with uncontrollable fury. The circumstances were these:

There was a man in Latium named Tyrrheus, who held the office of royal herdsman. He lived in his hut on some of the domains of Latinus, and had charge of the flocks and herds belonging to the king. He had two sons, and likewise a daughter. The daughter's name was Sylvia. The two boys had one day succeeded in making prisoner of a young stag, which they found in the woods with its mother. It was extremely young when they captured it, and they brought it home as a great prize They fed it with milk until it was old enough to take other food, and as it grew up accustomed to their hands, it was very tame and docile, and became a great favorite with all the family. Sylvia loved and played with it continually. She kept it always in trim by washing it in a fountain, and combing and smoothing its hair, and she amused herself by adorning it with wreaths, and garlands, and such other decorations as her sylvan resources could command.

One day when Ascanius, Æneas's son, who had now grown to be a young man, and who seems to have been characterized by a full share of the ardent and impulsive energy belonging to his years, was returning from the chase, he happened to pass by the place where the herdsman lived. Ascanius was followed by his dogs, and he had his bow and arrows in his hand. As he was thus passing along a copse of wood, near a brook, the dogs came suddenly upon Sylvia's stag. The confiding animal, unconscious of any danger, had strayed away from the herdsman's grounds to this grove, and had gone down to the brook to drink. The dogs immediately sprang upon him, in full cry. Ascanius followed, drawing at the same time an arrow from his quiver and fitting it to the bow. As soon as he came in sight of the stag, he let fly his arrow. The arrow pierced the poor fugitive in the side, and inflicted a dreadful wound. It did not, however, bring him down. The stag bounded on down the valley toward his home, as if to seek protection from Sylvia. He came rushing into the house, marking his way with blood, ran to the covert which

Sylvia had provided for his resting-place at night, and crouching down there he filled the whole dwelling with piteous bleatings and cries.

Silvia's Stag

As soon as Tyrrheus, the father of Sylvia, and the two young men, her brothers, knew who it was that had thus wantonly wounded their favorite, they were filled with indignation and rage. They went out and aroused the neighboring peasantry, who very easily caught the spirit of resentment and revenge which burned in the bosoms of Tyrrheus and his sons. They armed themselves with clubs, firebrands, scythes, and such other rustic weapons as came to hand, and rushed forth, resolved to punish the overbearing insolence of their foreign visitors, in the most summary manner.

In the mean time the Trojan youth, having heard the tidings of this disturbance, began to gather hastily, but in great numbers, to defend Ascanius. The parties on both sides were headstrong, and highly excited; and before any of the older and more considerate chieftains could interfere, a very serious conflict ensued. One of the sons of Tyrrheus was killed. He was pierced in the throat by an arrow, and fell and died immediately. His name was Almon. He was but a boy, or at all events had not yet arrived at years of maturity, and his premature and sudden death added greatly to the prevailing excitement. Another man too was killed. At length the conflict was brought to an end for the time but the excitement and the exasperation of the peasantry were extreme. They carried the two dead bodies in procession to the capital, to exhibit them to Latinus; and they demanded, in the most earnest and determined manner, that he should immediately make war upon the whole Trojan horde, and drive them back into the sea, whence they came.

Latinus found it extremely difficult to withstand this torrent. He remained firm for a time, and made every exertion in his power to quell the excitement and to pacify the minds of his people. But all was in vain. Public sentiment turned hopelessly against the Trojans, and Æneas soon found himself shut up in his city, surrounded with enemies, and left to his fate. Turnus was the leader of these foes.

He, however, did not despair. Both parties began to prepare vigorously for war. Æneas himself went away with a few followers to some of the neighboring kingdoms, to get succor from them. Neighboring states are almost always jealous of each other, and are easily induced to take part against each other, when involved in foreign wars. Æneas found several of the Italian princes who were ready to aid him, and he returned to his camp with considerable reinforcements, and with promises of more. The war soon broke out, and was waged for a long time with great determination on both sides and with varied success.

Latinus, who was now somewhat advanced in life, and had thus passed beyond the period of ambition and love of glory, and who besides must have felt that the interests of his family were now indissolubly bound up in those of Æneas and Lavinia, watched the progress of the contest with a very uneasy and anxious mind. He found that for a time at least it would be out of his power to do any thing effectual to terminate the war, so he allowed it to take its course, and contented himself with waiting patiently, in hopes that an occasion which would allow of his interposing with some hope of success, would sooner or later come.

Such an occasion did come; for after the war had been prosecuted for some time it was found, that notwithstanding the disadvantages under which the Trojans labored, they were rather gaining than losing ground. There were in fact some advantages as well as some disadvantages in their position. They formed a compact and concentrated body, while their enemies constituted a scattered population, spreading in a more or less exposed condition over a considerable extent of country. They had neither flocks nor herds, nor any other property for their enemies to plunder, while the Rutulians and Latins had great possessions, both of treasure in the towns and of rural produce in the country, so that when the Trojans gained the victory over them in any sally or foray, they always came home laden with booty, as well as exultant in triumph and pride; while if the Latins conquered the Trojans in a battle, they had nothing but the empty honor to reward them. The Trojans, too, were hardy, enduring, and indomitable. The alternative with them was victory or destruction. Their protracted voyage, and the long experience of hardships and sufferings which they had undergone, had inured them to privation and toil, so that they proved to the Latins and Rutulians to be very obstinate and formidable foes.

At length, as usual in such cases, indications gradually appeared that both sides began to be weary of the contest. Latinus availed himself of a favorable occasion which offered, to propose that embassadors should be sent to Æneas with terms of peace. Turnus was very much opposed to any such plan. He was earnestly desirous of continuing to prosecute the war. The other Latin chieftains reproached him then with being the cause of all the calamities which they were enduring, and urged the unreasonableness on his part of desiring any longer to protract the sufferings of his unhappy country, merely to gratify his own private resentment and revenge. Turnus ought not any longer to ask, they said, that others should fight in his quarrel; and they proposed that he should himself decide the question between him and Æneas, by challenging the Trojan leader to fight him in single combat.

Latinus strongly disapproved of this proposal. He was weary of war and bloodshed, and wished that the conflict might wholly cease; and he urged that peace should be made with Æneas, and that his original design of giving him Lavinia for his wife should be carried into execution. For a moment Turnus seemed to hesitate, but in looking towards Lavinia who, with Amata her mother, was present at this consultation, he saw, or thought he saw, in the agitation which she manifested, proofs of her love for him, and indications of a wish on her part that he and not Æneas should win her for his bride.

He accordingly without any farther hesitation or delay agreed to the proposal of the counsellor. The challenge to single combat was given and accepted, and on the appointed day the ground was marked out for the duel, and both armies were drawn up upon the field, to be spectators of the fight.

After the usual preparations the conflict began; but, as frequently occurs in such cases, it was not long confined to the single pair of combatants with which it commenced. Others were gradually drawn in, and the duel became in the end a general battle. Æneas and the Trojans were victorious, and both Latinus and Turnus were slain. This ended the war. Æneas married Lavinia, and thenceforth reigned with her over the kingdom of Latium as its rightful sovereign.

Æneas lived several years after this, and has the credit, in history, of having managed the affairs of the kingdom in a very wise and provident manner. He had brought with him from Troy the arts and the learning of the Greeks, and these he introduced to his people so as greatly to improve their condition. He introduced, too, many ceremonies of religious worship, which had prevailed in the countries from which he had come, or in those which he had visited in his long voyage. These ceremonies became at last so firmly established among the religious observances of the inhabitants of Latium, that they descended from generation to generation, and in subsequent years exercised great influence, in modeling the religious faith and worship of the Roman people. They thus continued to be practiced for many ages, and, through the literature of the Romans, became subsequently known and celebrated throughout the whole civilized world.

At length, in a war which Æneas was waging with the Rutulians, he was once, after a battle, reduced to great extremity of danger, and in order to escape from his pursuers he attempted to swim across a stream, and was drowned. The name of this stream was Numicius. It flowed into the sea a little north of Lavinium. It must have been larger in former times than it is now, for travelers who visit it at the present day say that it is now only a little rivulet, in which it would be almost impossible for any one to be drowned.

The Trojan followers of Æneas concealed his body, and spread the story among the people of Latium that he had been taken up to heaven. The people accordingly, having before considered their king as the son of a goddess, now looked upon him as himself divine. They accordingly erected altars to him in Latium and thenceforth worshiped him as a God.

7

Rhea Silvia

RHEA SILVIA, the mother of Romulus, was a vestal virgin, who lived in the kingdom of Latium about four hundred years after the death of Æneas. A vestal virgin was a sort of priestess, who was required, like the nuns of modern times, to live in seclusion from the rest of the world, and devote their time wholly and without reserve to the services of religion. They were, like nuns, especially prohibited from all association and intercourse with men.

Æneas himself is said to have founded the order of vestal virgins, and to have instituted the rites and services which were committed to their charge. These rites and services were in honor of Vesta, who was the goddess of Home. The fireside has been, in all ages and countries, the center and the symbol of home, and the worship of Vesta consisted, accordingly, of ceremonies designed to dignify and exalt the fireside in the estimation of the people. Instead of the images and altars which were used in the worship of the other deities, a representation of a fire-stand was made, such as were used in the houses of those days; and upon this sacred stand a fire was kept continually burning, and various rites and ceremonies were performed in connection with it, in honor of the domestic virtues and enjoyments, of which it was the type and symbol.

These fire-stands, as used by the ancients, were very different from the fire-places of modern times, which are recesses in chimneys with flues above for the passage of the smoke. The household fires of the ancients were placed in the center of the apartment, on a hearth or supporter called the focus. This hearth was made sometimes of stone or brick, and sometimes of bronze. The smoke escaped above, through openings in the roof. This would seem, according to the ideas of the present day, a very comfortless arrangement; but it must be remembered that the climate in those countries was mild, and there was accordingly but little occasion for fire; and then, besides, such were the habits of the people at this period of the world, that not only their pursuits and avocations, but far the greater portion of their pleasures, called them into the open air. Still, the fire-place was, with them as with us, the type and emblem of domestic life; and accordingly, in paying divine honors to Vesta, the goddess of Home, they set up a focus, or fire-place, in her temple, instead of an altar, and in the place of sacrifices they simply kept burning upon it a perpetual fire.

The priestesses who had charge of the fire were selected for this purpose when they were children. It was required that they should be from six to ten years of age. When chosen they were consecrated to the service of Vesta by the most solemn ceremonies, and as virgins, were bound under awful penalties, to spotless purity of life. As the perpetual fire in the temple of Vesta represented the fire of the domestic hearth, so these vestal virgins represented the maidens by whom the domestic service of a household is performed; and the life of seclusion and celibacy which was required of them was the emblem of the innocence and purity which the institution of the family is expressly intended to guard. The duties of the vestals were analogous to those of domestic maidens. They were to watch the fire, and never to allow it to go out. They were to perform various rites and ceremonies connected with the worship of Vesta and to keep the interior of the temple and the shrines pure and clean, and the sacred vessels and utensils arranged, as in a well-ordered household. In a word, they were to be, in purity, in industry, in neatness, in order, and in patience and vigilance, the perfect impersonation of maidenly virtue as exhibited in its own proper field of duty at home.

The most awful penalties were visited upon the head of any vestal virgin who was guilty of violating her vows. There is no direct evidence what these penalties were at this early period, but in subsequent years, at Rome, where the vestal virgins resided, the man who was guilty of enticing one of them away from her duty was publicly scourged to death in the Roman forum. For the vestal herself, thus led away, a cell was dug beneath the ground, and vaulted over. A pit led down to this subterranean dungeon, entering it by one side. In the dungeon itself there was placed a table, a lamp, and a little food. The descent was by a ladder which passed down through the pit. The place of this terrible preparation for punishment was near one of the gates of the city, and when all was ready the unhappy vestal was brought forth, at the head of a great public procession,—she herself being attended by her friends and relatives, all mourning and lamenting her fate by the way. The ceremony, in a word, was in all respects a funeral, except that the person who was to be buried was still alive. On arriving at the spot, the wretched criminal was conducted down the ladder and placed upon the couch in the cell. The assistants who performed this service then returned; the ladder was drawn up; earth was thrown in until the pit was filled; and the erring girl was left to her fate, which was, when her lamp had burned out, and her food was expended, to starve by slow degrees, and die at last in darkness and despair.

If we would do full justice to the ancient founders of civilization and empire, we should probably consider their enshrinement of Vesta, and the contriving of the ceremonies and observances which were instituted in honor of her, not as the setting up of an idol or false god, for worship, in the sense in which Christian nations worship the spiritual and eternal Jehovah—but rather as the embodiment of an idea,—a principle,—as the best means, in those rude ages, of attracting to it the general regard.

Even in our own days, and in Christian lands, men erect a pole in honor of liberty, and surmount it with the image of a cap. And if, instead of the cap, they were to place a carved effigy of liberty above, and to assemble for periodical celebrations below, with games, and music, and banners, we should not probably call them idolaters. So Christian poets write odes and invocations to Peace, to Disappointment, to Spring, to Beauty, in which they impersonate an idea, or a principle, and address it in the language of adoration, as if it were a sentient being, possessing magical and mysterious powers. In the same manner, the rites and celebrations of ancient times are not necessarily all to be considered as idolatry, and denounced as inexcusably wicked and absurd. Our fathers set up an image in honor of liberty, to strengthen the influence of the love of liberty on the popular mind. It is possible that Æneas looked upon the subject in the same light, in erecting a public fireside in honor of domestic peace and happiness, and in designating maidens to guard it with constant vigilance and with spotless purity. At all events, the institution exercised a vast and an incalculable power, in impressing the minds of men, in those rude ages, with a sense of the sacredness of the domestic tie, and in keeping before their minds a high standard, in theory at least, of domestic honor and purity. We must remember that they had not then the word of God, nor any means of communicating to the minds of the people any general enlightenment and instruction. They were obliged, therefore, to resort to the next best method which their ingenuity could devise.

There were a great many very extraordinary rites and ceremonies connected with the service of the vestal altar, and many singular regulations for the conduct of it, the origin and design of which it would now be very difficult to ascertain. As has already been remarked, the virgins were chosen when very young, being, when designated to the office, not under six nor over ten years of age. They were chosen by the king, and it was necessary that the candidate, besides the above-named requisite in regard to age, should be in a perfect condition of soundness and health in respect to all her bodily limbs and members, and also to the faculties of her mind. It was required too that she should be the daughter of free and freeborn parents, who had never been in slavery, and had never followed any menial or degrading occupation; and also that both her parents should be living. To be an orphan was considered, it seems, in some sense an imperfection.

The service of the vestal virgins continued for thirty years; and when this period had expired, the maidens were discharged from their vows, and were allowed, if they chose, to lay aside their vestal robes, and the other emblems of their office, and return to the world, with the privilege even of marrying, if they chose to do so. Though the laws however permitted this, there was a public sentiment against it, and it was seldom that any of the vestal priestesses availed themselves of the privilege. They generally remained after their term of service had expired, in attendance at the temple, and died as they had lived in the service of the goddess.

One of the chief functions of the virgins, in their service in the temple, was to keep the sacred fire perpetually burning. This fire was never to go out, and if, by any neglect on the part of the vestal in attendance, this was allowed to occur, the guilty maiden was punished terribly by scourging. The punishment was inflicted by the hands of the highest pontifical officer of the state. The laws of the institution however evinced their high regard for the purity and modesty of the vestal maidens by requiring that the blows should be administered in the dark, the sufferer having been previously prepared to receive them by being partially undressed by her female attendants. The extinguished fire was then rekindled with many solemn ceremonies.

Rhea Silvia, the mother of Romulus, was, we repeat, a vestal virgin. She lived four hundred years after the death of Æneas. During these four centuries, the kingdom had been governed by the descendants of Æneas, generally in a peaceful and prosperous manner, although some difficulties occurred in the establishment of the succession immediately after Æneas's death. It will be remembered that Æneas was drowned during the continuance of the war. He left one son, and perhaps others. The one who figured most conspicuously in the subsequent history of the kingdom, was Ascanius, the son who had accompanied Æneas from Troy, and who had now attained to years of maturity. He, of course, on his father's death, immediately succeeded him.

There was some question, however, whether, after all, Lavinia herself was not entitled to the kingdom. It was doubtful, according to the laws and usages of those days, whether Æneas held the realm in his own right, or as the husband of Lavinia, who was the daughter and heir of Latinus, the ancient and legitimate king. Lavinia, however, seemed to have no disposition to assert her claim. She was of a mild and gentle spirit; and, besides, her health was at that time such as to lead her to wish for retirement and repose. She even had some fears for her personal safety, not knowing but that Ascanius would be suspicious and jealous of her on account of her claims to the throne, and that he might be tempted to do her some injury. Her husband had been her only protector among the Trojans, and now, since he was no more, and another, who was in some sense her rival, had risen to power, she naturally felt insecure. She accordingly took the first opportunity to retire from Lavinium. She went away into the forests in the interior of the country, with a very few attendants and friends, and concealed herself there in a safe retreat. The family that received and sheltered her, was that of Tyrrheus, the chief of her father's shepherds, whose children's stag Ascanius had formerly killed. Here, in a short time, she had a son. She determined to name him from his father; and in order to commemorate his having been born in the midst of the wild forest scenes which surrounded her at the time of his birth, she called him in full, Æneas of the woods, or, as it was expressed in the language which was then used in Latium, Æneas Silvius. The boy, when he grew up, was always known by this name in subsequent history.

And not only did he himself retain the name, but he transmitted it to his posterity, for all the kings that afterward descended from him, extending in a long line through a period of four hundred years, had the word Silvius affixed to their names, in perpetual commemoration of the romantic birth of their ancestor. Rhea, the mother of Romulus, of whom we have already spoken, of and whom we shall presently have occasion to speak still more, was Rhea Silvia, by reason of her having been by birth a princess of this royal line.

Ascanius, in the mean time, on the death of his father, was for a time so engrossed in the prosecution of the war, that he paid but little attention to the departure of Lavinia. The name of the king of the Rutulians who fought against him was Mezentius. Mezentius had a son named Lausus, and both father and son were personally serving in the army by which Ascanius was besieged in Lavinium. Mezentius had command in the camp, at the head-quarters of the army, which was at some distance from the city. Lausus headed an advanced guard, which had established itself strongly at a post which they had taken near the gates. In this state of things, Ascanius, one dark and stormy night, planned a sortie. He organized a desperate body of followers, and after watching the flashes of lightning for a time, to find omens from them indicating success, he gave the signal. The gates were opened and the column of armed men sallied forth, creeping noiselessly forward in the darkness and gloom, until they came to the encampment of Lausus. They fell upon this camp with an irresistible rush, and with terrific shouts and outcries. The whole detachment were taken entirely by surprise, and great numbers were made prisoners or slain. Lausus himself was killed.

Excited by their victory, the Trojan soldiers, headed by Ascanius, now turned their course toward the main body of the Rutulian army. Mezentius had, however, in the mean time, obtained warning of their approach, and when they reached his camp he was ready to retreat. He fled with all his forces toward the mountains. Ascanius and the Trojans followed him. Mezentius halted and attempted to fortify himself on a hill. Ascanius surrounded the hill, and soon compelled his enemies to come to terms. A treaty was made, and Mezentius and his forces soon after withdrew from the country, leaving Ascanius and Latium in peace.

Ascanius then, after having in some degree settled his affairs, began to think of Lavinia. In fact, the Latian portion of his subjects seemed disposed to murmur and complain, at her having been compelled to withdraw from her own paternal kingdom, in order to leave the throne to the occupancy of the son of a stranger. Some even feared that she had come to some harm, or that Ascanius might in the end put her to death when time had been allowed for the recollection of her to pass in some degree from the minds of men. So the public began generally to call for Lavinia's return.

Ascanius seems to have been well disposed to do justice in the case, for he not only sought out Lavinia and induced her to return to the capital with her little son, but he finally concluded to give up Lavinium to her entirely, as her own rightful dominion, while he went away and founded a new city for himself. He accordingly explored the country around for a favorable site, and at length decided upon a spot nearly north of Lavinium, and not many miles distant from it. The place which he marked out for the walls of the city was at the foot of a mountain, on a tract of somewhat elevated ground, which formed one of the lower declivities of it. The mountain, rising abruptly on one side, formed a sure defense on that side: on the other side was a small lake, of clear and pellucid water. In front, and somewhat below, there were extended plains of fertile land. Ascanius, after having determined on this place as the site of his intended city, set his men at work to make the necessary constructions. Some built the walls of the city, and laid out streets and erected houses within. Others were employed in forming the declivity of the mountain above into terraces, for the cultivation of the vine. The slopes which they thus graded had a southern exposure, and the grapes which subsequently grew there, were luxurious and delicious in flavor. From the little lake channels were cut leading over the plains below, and by this means a constant supply of water could be conveyed to the fields of grain which were to be sown there, for purposes of irrigation. Thus the place which Ascanius chose furnished all possible facilities both for maintaining, and also for defending the people who were to make it their abode. The town was called Alba Longa, that is long Alba. It was called long to distinguish it from another Alba. It was really long in its form, as the buildings extended for a considerable distance along the border of the lake.

Ascanius reigned over thirty years at Alba Longa, while Lavinia reigned at Lavinium, each friendly to the other and governing the country at large, together, in peace and harmony. In process of time both died. Ascanius left a son whose name was Iulus, while Æneas Silvius was Lavinia's heir.

There was, of course, great diversity of opinion throughout the nation in regard to the comparative claims of these two princes respectively. Some maintained that Æneas the Trojan became, by conquest, the rightful sovereign of Latium, irrespective of any rights that he acquired through his marriage with Lavinia, and that Iulus, as the son of his eldest son, rightfully succeeded him. Others contended that Lavinia represented the ancient and the truly legitimate royal line, and that Æneas Silvius, as her son and heir, ought to be placed upon the throne. And there were those who proposed to compromise the question, by dividing Latium into two separate kingdoms, giving up one part to Iulus, with Alba Longa for its capital, and the other, with Lavinium for its capital, to Æneas Silvius, Lavinia's heir. This proposition was, however, overruled. The two kingdoms, thus formed would be small and feeble, it was thought, and unable to defend themselves against the other Italian nations in case of war. The question was finally settled by a different sort of compromise. It was agreed that Latium should retain its integrity, and that Æneas Silvius, being the son both of Æneas and Lavinia, and thus representing both branches of the reigning power, should be the king, while Iulus and his descendants forever, should occupy the position, scarcely less inferior, of sovereign power in matters of religion. Æneas Silvius, therefore, and his descendants, became kings, and as such commanded the armies and directed the affairs of state, while Iulus and his family were exalted, in connection with them, to the highest pontifical dignities.

This state of things, once established, continued age after age, and century after century, for about four hundred years. No records, and very few traditions in respect to what occurred during this period remain. One circumstance, however, took place which caused itself to be remembered. There was one king in the line of the Silvii, whose name was Tiberinus. In one of his battles with the armies of the nation adjoining him on the northern side, he attempted to swim across the river that formed the frontier. He was forced down by the current, and was seen no more. By the accident, however, he gave the name of Tiber to the stream, and thus perpetuated his own memory through the subsequent renown of the river in which he was drowned. Before this time the river was called the Albula.

Another incident is related, which is somewhat curious, as illustrating the ideas and customs of the times. One of this Silvian line of sovereigns was named Alladius. This Alladius conceived the idea of making the people believe that he was a god, and in order to accomplish this end he resorted to the contrivance of imitating, by artificial means, the sound of the rumbling of thunder and the flashes of lightning at night from his palace on the banks of the lake at Alba Longa. He employed, probably, for this purpose some means similar to those resorted to for the same end in theatrical spectacles at the present day. The people, however were not deceived by this imposture, though they soon after fell into an error nearly as absurd as believing in this false thunder would have been; for, on an occasion which occurred not long afterward, probably that of a great storm accompanied with torrents of rain upon the mountains around, the lake rose so high as to produce an inundation, in which the water broke into the palace, and the pretended thunderer was drowned. The people considered that he was destroyed thus by the special interposition of heaven, to punish him for his impiety in daring to assume what was then considered the peculiar attribute and prerogative of supreme divinity. In fact, the rumor circulated, and one historian has recorded it as true, that Alladius was struck by the lightning which accompanied the storm, and thus killed at once by the terrible agency which he had presumed to counterfeit, before the inundation of the palace came on. If he met his death in any sudden and unusual manner, it is not at all surprising that his fate should have been attributed to the judgment of God, for thunder was regarded in those days with an extreme and superstitious veneration and awe. All this is, however, now changed. Men have learned to understand thunder, and to protect themselves from its power; and now, since Franklin and Morse have commenced the work of subduing the potent and mysterious agent in which it originates, to the human will, the presumption is not very strong against the supposition that the time may come when human science may actually produce it in the sky—as it is now produced, in effect, upon the lecturer's table.

At last, toward the close of the four hundred years during which the dynasty of the Silvii continued to reign over Latium, a certain monarch of the series died, leaving two children, Numitor and Amulius. Numitor was the eldest son, and as such entitled to succeed his father. But he was of a quiet and somewhat inefficient disposition, while his younger brother was ardent and ambitious, and very likely to aspire to the possession of power. The father, it seems, anticipated the possibility of dissension between his sons after his death, and in order to do all in his power to guard against it, he endeavored to arrange and settle the succession before he died. In the course of the negotiations which ensued, Amulius proposed that his father's possessions should be divided into two portions, the kingdom to constitute one, and the wealth and treasures the other, and that Numitor should choose which portion he would have. This proposal seemed to have the appearance, at least, of reasonableness and impartiality; and it would have been really very reasonable, if the right to the inheritance thus disposed of, had belonged equally to the younger and to the elder son. But it did not. And thus the offer of Amulius was, in effect, a proposition to divide with himself that which really belonged wholly to his brother.

Numitor, however, who, it seems, was little disposed to contend for his rights, agreed to this proposal. He, however, chose the kingdom, and left the wealth for his brother; and the inheritance was accordingly thus divided on the death of the father. But Amulius, as soon as he came into possession of his treasures, began to employ them as a means of making powerful friends, and strengthening his political influence. In due time he usurped the throne, and Numitor, giving up the contest with very little attempt to resist the usurpation, fled and concealed himself in some obscure place of retreat. He had, however, two children, a son and a daughter, which he left behind him in his flight. Amulius feared that these children might, at some future time, give him trouble, by advancing claims as their father's heirs. He did not dare to kill them openly, for fear of exciting the popular odium against himself. He was obliged, therefore, to resort to stratagem.

The son, whose name was Egestus, he caused to be slain at a hunting party, by employing remorseless and desperate men to shoot him, in the heat of the chase, with arrows, or thrust him through with a spear, watching their opportunity for doing this at a moment when they were not observed, or when it might appear to be an accident. The daughter, whose name was Rhea—the Rhea Silvia named at the commencement of this chapter—he could not well actually destroy, without being known to be her murderer; and perhaps too, he had enough remaining humanity to be unwilling to shed the blood of a helpless and beautiful maiden, the daughter, too, of his own brother. Then, besides, he had a daughter of his own named Antho, who was the playmate and companion of Rhea, and with whose affection for her cousin he must have felt some sympathy. He would not, therefore, destroy the child, but contented himself with determining to make her a vestal virgin. By this means she would be solemnly set apart to a religious service, which would incapacitate her from aspiring to the throne; and by being cut off, by her vestal vows, from all possibility of forming any domestic ties, she could never, he thought, have any offspring to dispute his claim to the throne.

There was nothing very extraordinary in this consecration of his niece, princess as she was, to the service of the vestal fire; for it had been customary for children of the highest rank to be designated to this office. The little Rhea, for she was yet a child when her uncle took this determination in respect to her, made, as would appear, no objection to what she perhaps considered a distinguished honor. The ceremonies, therefore, of her consecration were duly performed; she took the vows, and bound herself by the most awful sanctions—unconscious, however, perhaps, herself of what she was doing—to lead thenceforth a life of absolute celibacy and seclusion.

She was then received into the temple of Vesta, and there, with the other maidens who had been consecrated before her, she devoted herself to the discharge of the duties of her office, without reproach, for several years. At length, however, certain circumstances occurred, which suddenly terminated Rhea's career as a vestal virgin, and led to results of the most momentous character.

What these circumstances were, will be explained in the next chapter.

8

The Twins

ALTHOUGH the temple of Vesta itself, at Alba Longa, was the principal scene of the duties which devolved upon the vestal virgins, still they were not wholly confined in their avocations to that sacred edifice, but were often called upon, one or two at a time, to perform services, or to assist in the celebration of rites, at other places in the city and vicinity.

There was a temple consecrated to Mars near to Alba. It was situated in an opening in the woods, in some little glen or valley at the base of the mountain. There was a stream of water running through the ground, and Rhea in the performance of her duties as a vestal was required at one time to pass to and fro through the groves in this solitary place to fetch water. Here she allowed herself, in violation of her vestal vows, to form the acquaintance of a man, whom she met in the groves. She knew well that by doing so she made herself subject to the most dreadful penalties in case her fault should become known. Still she yielded to the temptation, and allowed herself to be persuaded to remain with the stranger. She said afterward, when the facts were brought to light, that her meeting with this companion was wholly unintentional on her part. She saw a wolf in the grove, she said, and she ran terrified into a cave to escape from him, and that the man came to her there, to protect her, and then compelled her to remain with him. Besides, from his dress, and countenance, and air, she had believed him, she said, to be the God Mars himself, and thought that it was not her duty to resist his will.

Rhea Silvia

However this may be, her stolen interview or interviews with this stranger were not known at the time, and Rhea perhaps thought that her fault would never be discovered. Some weeks after this, however, it was observed by her companions and friends that she began to appear thoughtful and depressed. Her dejection increased day by day; her face became wan and pale, and her eyes were often filled with tears. They asked her what was the cause of her trouble. She said that she was sick. She was soon afterward excused from her duties in the Vestal temple, and went away, and remained for some time shut up in retirement and seclusion. There at length two children, twins, were born to her.

It was only through the influence of Antho, Rhea's cousin, that the unhappy vestal was not put to death by Amulius, before her children were born, at the time when her fault was first discovered. The laws of the State in respect to vestal virgins, which were inexorably severe, would have justified him in causing her to be executed at once, but Antho interceded so earnestly for her unhappy cousin, that Amulius for a time spared her life. When, however, her sons were born, the anger of Amulius broke out anew. If she had remained childless he would probably have allowed her to live, though she could of course never have been restored to her office in the temple of Vesta. Or if she had given birth to a daughter she might have been pardoned, since a daughter, on account of her sex, would have been little likely to disturb Amulius in the possession of the kingdom. But the existence of two sons, born directly in the line of the succession, and each of them having claims superior to his own, endangered, most imminently, he perceived, his possession of power. He was of course greatly enraged.

He caused Rhea to be shut up in close imprisonment, and as for the boys, he ordered them to be thrown into the Tiber. The Tiber was at some considerable distance from Alba; but it was probably near the place where Rhea had resided in her retirement, and where the children were born.

A peasant of that region was intrusted with the task of throwing the children into the river. Whether his official duty in undertaking this commission required him actually to drown the boys, or whether he was allowed to give the helpless babes some little chance for their lives, is not known. At all events he determined that in committing the children to the stream he would so arrange it that they should float away from his sight, in order that he might not himself be a witness of their dying struggles and cries. He accordingly put them upon a species of float that he made,—a sort of box or trough, as would seem from the ancient descriptions, which he had hollowed out from a log,—and disposing their little limbs carefully within this narrow receptacle, he pushed the frail boat, with its navigators still more frail, out upon the current of the river.

The name of the peasant who performed this task was Faustulus. The peasant also who subsequently,—as will hereafter appear,—found and took charge of the children, is spoken of by the ancient historians as Faustulus, too. In fact we might well suppose that no man, however rustic and rude, could give his time and his thoughts to two such babes long enough to make an ark for them, for the purpose of making it possible to save their lives, and then place them carefully in it to send them away, without becoming so far interested in their fate, and so touched by their mute and confiding helplessness, as to feel prompted to follow the stream to see how so perilous a navigation would end. We have, however, no direct evidence that Faustulus did so watch the progress of his boat down the river. The story is that it was drifted along, now whirling in eddies, and now shooting down over rapid currents, until at last, at a bend in the river, it was thrown upon the beach, and being turned over by the concussion, the children were rolled out upon the sand.

The neighboring thickets soon of course resounded with their plaintive cries. A mother wolf who was sleeping there came out to see what was the matter. Now a mother, of whatever race, is irresistibly drawn by an instinct, if incapable of a sentiment, of affection, to love and to cherish any thing that is newly born. The wolf caressed the helpless babes, imagining perhaps that they were her own offspring; and lying down by their side she cherished and fed them, watching all the time with a fierce and vigilant eye for any approaching enemy or danger. The rude nursery might very naturally be supposed to be in dangerous proximity to the water, but it happened that the river, when the babes were set adrift in it, was very high, from the effect of rains upon the mountains, and thus soon after the children were thrown upon the land, the water began to subside. In a short time it wholly returned to its accustomed channel, leaving the children on the warm sand, high above all danger. The wolf was not their only guardian. A woodpecker, the tradition says, watched over them too, and brought them berries and other sylvan food. The reader will perhaps be disposed to hesitate a little in receiving this last statement for sober history, but as no part of the whole narrative will bear any very rigid scrutiny, we may as well take the story of the woodpecker along with the rest.

Faustulus and the Twins

In a short time the children were rescued from their exposed situation by a shepherd, who is called Faustulus, and may or may not have been the same with the Faustulus by whom they had been exposed. Faustulus carried the children to his hut; and there the maternal attentions of the wolf and the woodpecker were replaced by those of the shepherd's wife. Her name was Larentia. Faustulus was one of Amulius's herdsmen, having the care of the flocks and herds that grazed on this part of the royal domain, but living, like any other shepherd, in great seclusion, in his hut in the forests. He not only rescued the children, but he brought home and preserved the trough in which they had been floated down the river. He put this relic aside, thinking that the day might perhaps come in which there would be occasion to produce it. He told the story of the children only to a very few trustworthy friends, and he accompanied the communication, in the cases where he made it, with many injunctions of secrecy. He named the foundlings Romulus and Remus, and as they grew up they passed generally for the shepherd's sons.

Faustulus felt a great degree of interest, and a high sense of responsibility too, in having these young princes under his care. He took great pains to protect them from all possible harm, and to instruct them in every thing which it was in those days considered important for young men to know. It is even said that he sent them to a town in Latium where there was some sort of seminary of learning, that their minds might receive a proper intellectual culture. As they grew up they were both handsome in form and in countenance, and were characterized by a graceful dignity of air and demeanor, which made them very attractive in the eyes of all who beheld them. They were prominent among the young herdsmen and hunters of the forest, for their courage, their activity, their strength, their various personal accomplishments, and their high and generous qualities of mind. Romulus was more silent and thoughtful than his brother, and seemed to possess in some respects superior mental powers. Both were regarded by all who knew them with feelings of the highest respect and consideration.

Romulus and Remus treated their own companions and equals, that is the young shepherds and herdsmen of the mountains, with great courtesy and kindness, and were very kindly regarded by them in return. They, however, evinced a great degree of independence of spirit in respect to the various bailiffs and chief herdsmen, and other officers of field and forest police, who exercised authority in the region where they lived. These men were sometimes haughty and domineering, and the peasantry in general stood greatly in awe of them. Romulus and Remus, however, always faced them without fear, never seeming to be alarmed at their threats, or at any other exhibitions of their anger. In fact, the boys seemed to be imbued with a native loftiness and fearlessness of character, as if they had inherited a spirit of confidence and courage with their royal blood, or had imbibed a portion of the indomitable temper of their fierce foster mother.

They were generous, however, as well as brave. They took the part of the weak and the oppressed against the tyrannical and the strong in the rustic contentions that they witnessed; they interposed to help the feeble, to relieve those who were in want, and to protect the defenseless. They hunted wild beasts, they fought against robbers, they rescued and saved the lost. For amusements, they practiced running, wrestling, racing, throwing javelins and spears, and other athletic feats and accomplishments—in every thing excelling all their competitors, and becoming in the end greatly renowned.

Numitor, the father of Rhea Silvia, whom Amulius had dethroned and banished from Alba, was all this time still living; and he had now at length become so far reconciled to Amulius as to be allowed to reside in Alba—though he lived there as a private citizen. He owned, it seems, some estates near the Tiber, where he had flocks and herds that were tended by his shepherds and herdsmen. It happened at one time that some contention arose between the herdsmen of Numitor and those of Amulius, among whom Romulus and Remus were residing. Now as the young men had thus far, of course, no idea whatever of their relationship to Numitor, there was no reason why they should feel any special interest in his affairs, and they accordingly, as might naturally have been expected, took part with Amulius in this quarrel, since Faustulus, and all the shepherds around them were on that side. The herdsmen of Numitor in the course of the quarrel drove away some of the cattle which were claimed as belonging to the herdsmen of Amulius. Romulus and Remus headed a band which they hastily called together, to pursue the depredators and bring the cattle back. They succeeded in this expedition, and recaptured the herd. This incensed the party of Numitor and they determined on revenge.

They waited some time for a favorable opportunity. At length the time came for celebrating a certain festival called the Supercalia, which consisted of very rude games and ceremonies, in which men sacrificed goats, and then dressed themselves partially in the skins, and ran about whipping every one whom they met, with thongs made likewise of the skins of goats, or of rabbits, or other animals remarkable for their fecundity. The meaning of the ceremonies, so far as such uncouth and absurd ceremonies could have any meaning, was to honor the God of fertility and fruitfulness, and to promote the fruitfulness of their flocks and herds, during the year ensuing at the time that the celebrations were held.

The retainers and partisans of Numitor determined on availing themselves of this opportunity to accomplish their object. Accordingly, they armed themselves, and coming suddenly upon the spot where the shepherds of Amulius were celebrating the games, they made a rush for Remus, who was at that time, in accordance with the custom, running to and fro, half-naked, and armed only with goat-skin thongs. They succeeded in making him prisoner, and bore him away in triumph to Numitor.

Of course, this daring act produced great excitement throughout the country. Numitor was well pleased with the prize that he had secured, but felt, at the same time, some fear of the responsibility which he incurred by holding the prisoner. He was strongly inclined to proceed against Remus, and punish him himself for the offenses which the herdsmen of his lands charged against him; but he finally concluded that this would not be safe, and he determined, in the end, to refer the case to Amulius for decision. He accordingly sent Remus to Amulius, making grievous charges against him, as a lawless desperado, who, with his brother, Numitor said, were the terror of the forests, through their domineering temper and their acts of robbery and rapine.

The king, pleased, perhaps, with the spirit of deference to his regal authority on the part of his brother, implied in the referring of the case of the accused to him for trial, sent Remus back again to Numitor, saying that Numitor might punish the freebooter himself in any way that he thought best. Remus was accordingly brought again to Numitor's house. In the mean time, the fact of his being thus made a prisoner, and charged with crime, and the proceedings in relation to him, in sending him back and forth between Amulius and Numitor, strongly attracted public attention. Every one was talking of the prisoner, and discussing the question of his probable fate. The general interest which was thus awakened in respect to him and to his brother Romulus, revived the slumbering recollections in the minds of the old neighbors of Faustulus, of the stories which he had told them of his having found the twins on the bank of the river, in their infancy. They told this story to Romulus, and he or some other friends made it known to Remus while he was still confined.

When Remus was brought before Numitor—who was really his grandfather, though the fact of this relationship was wholly unknown to both of them—Numitor was exceedingly struck with his handsome countenance and form, and with his fearless and noble demeanor. The young prisoner seemed perfectly self-possessed and at his ease; and though he knew well that his life was at stake, there was a certain air of calmness and composure in his manner which seemed to denote very lofty qualities, both of person and mind.

A vague recollection of the lost children of his daughter Rhea immediately flashed across Numitor's mind. It changed all his anger against Remus to a feeling of wondering interest and curiosity, and gave to his countenance, as he looked upon his prisoner, an expression of kind and tender regard. After a short pause Numitor addressed the young captive —speaking in a gentle and conciliating manner—and asked him who he was, and who his parents were.

"I will frankly tell you all that I know," said Remus, "since you treat me in so fair and honorable a manner. The king delivered me up to be punished, without listening to what I had to say, but you seem willing to hear before you condemn. My name is Remus, and I have a twin-brother named Romulus. We have always supposed ourselves to be the children of Faustulus; but now, since this difficulty has occurred, we have heard new tidings in respect to our origin. We are told that we were found in our infancy, on the shore of the river, at the place where Faustulus lives, and that near by there was a box or trough, in which we had been floated down to the spot from a place above. When Faustulus found us, there was a wolf and a woodpecker taking care of us and bringing us food. Faustulus carried us to his house, and brought us up as his children. He preserved the trough, too, and has it now."

Numitor was, of course, greatly excited at hearing this intelligence. He perceived at once that the finding of these children, both in respect to time and place, and to all the attendant circumstances, corresponded so precisely with the exposure of the children of Rhea Silvia as to leave no reasonable ground for doubt that Romulus and Remus were his grandsons. He resolved immediately to communicate this joyful discovery to his daughter, if he could contrive the means of gaining access to her; for during all this time she had been kept in close confinement in her prison.

In the mean time, Romulus himself, at the house of Faustulus, in the forests, had become greatly excited by the circumstances in which he found himself placed. He had been first very much incensed at the capture of Remus, and while concerting with Faustulus plans for rescuing him, Faustulus had explained to him the mystery of his birth. He had informed him not only how he was found with his brother, on the bank of the river, but also had made known to him whose sons he and Remus were. Romulus was, of course, extremely elated at this intelligence. His native courage and energy were quickened anew by his learning that he and his brother were princes, and as he believed, rightfully entitled to the throne. He immediately began to form plans for raising a rebellion against the government of Amulius, with a view of first rescuing Remus from his power, and afterward taking such ulterior steps as circumstances might require.

Faustulus, on the other hand, leaving Romulus to raise the forces for his insurrection as he pleased, determined to go himself to Numitor and reveal the secret of the birth of Romulus and Remus to him. In order to confirm and corroborate his story, he took the trough with him, carrying it under his cloak, in order to conceal it from view, and in this manner made his appearance at the gates of Alba.

There was something in his appearance and manner when he arrived at the gate, which attracted the attention of the officers on guard there. He wore the dress of a countryman, and had obviously come in from the forests, a long way; and there was something in his air which denoted hurry and agitation. The soldiers asked him what he had under his cloak, and compelled him to produce the ark to view. The curiosity of the guardsmen was still more strongly aroused at seeing this old relic. It was bound with brass bands, and it had some rude inscription marked upon it. It happened that one of the guard was an old soldier who had been in some way connected with the exposure of the children of Rhea when they were set adrift in the river, and he immediately recognized this trough as the float which they had been placed in. He immediately concluded that some very extraordinary movement was going on,—and he determined to proceed forthwith and inform Amulius of what he had discovered. He accordingly went to the king and informed him that a man had been intercepted at the gate of the city, who was attempting to bring in, concealed under his cloak, the identical ark or float, which to his certain knowledge had been used in the case of the children of Rhea Silvia, for sending them adrift on the waters of the Tiber.

The king was greatly excited and agitated at receiving this intelligence. He ordered Faustulus to be brought into his presence. Faustulus was much terrified at receiving this summons. He had but little time to reflect what to say, and during the few minutes that elapsed while they were conducting him into the presence of the king, he found it hard to determine how much it would be best for him to admit, and how much to deny. Finally, in answer to the interrogations of the king, he acknowledged that he found the children and the ark in which they had been drifted upon the shore, and that he had saved the boys alive, and had brought them up as his children. He said, however, that he did not know where they were. They had gone away, he alledged, some years before, and were now living as shepherds in some distant part of the country, he did not know exactly where.

Amulius then asked Faustulus what he had been intending to do with the trough, which he was bringing so secretly into the city. Faustulus said that he was going to carry it to Rhea in her prison, she having often expressed a strong desire to see it, as a token or memorial which would recall the dear babes that had lain in it very vividly to her mind.

Amulius seemed satisfied that these statements were honest and true, but they awakened in his mind a very great solicitude and anxiety. He feared that the children, being still alive, might some day come to the knowledge of their origin, and so disturb his possession of the throne, and perhaps revenge, by some dreadful retaliation, the wrongs and injuries which he had inflicted upon their mother and their grandfather. The people, he feared, would be very much inclined to take part with them, and not with him, in any contest which might arise; for their sympathies were already on the side of Numitor. In a word, he was greatly alarmed, and he was much at a loss to know what to do, to avert the danger which was impending over him.

He concluded to send to Numitor and inquire of him whether he was aware that the boys were still alive, and if so, if he knew where they were to be found. He accordingly sent a messenger to his brother, commissioned to make these inquiries. This messenger, though in the service of Amulius, was really a friend to Numitor, and on being admitted to Numitor's presence, when he went to make the inquiries as directed by the king, he found Remus there,—though not, as he had expected, in the attitude of a prisoner awaiting sentence from a judge, but rather in that of a son in affectionate consultation with his father. He soon learned the truth, and immediately expressed his determination to espouse the cause of the prince. "The whole city will be on your side," said he to Remus. "You have only to place yourself at the head of the population, and proclaim your rights; and you will easily be restored to the possession of them."

Just at this crisis a tumult was heard at the gates of the city. Romulus had arrived there at the head of the band of peasants and herdsmen that he had collected in the forests. These insurgents were rudely armed and were organized in a very simple and primitive manner. For weapons the peasants bore such implements of agriculture as could be used for weapons, while the huntsmen brought their pikes, and spears, and javelins, and such other projectiles as were employed in those days in hunting wild beasts. The troop was divided into companies of one hundred, and for banners they bore tufts of grass on wisps of straw, or fern, or other herbage, tied at the top of a pole. The armament was rude, but the men were resolute and determined, and they made their appearance at the gates of the city upon the outside, just in time to co-operate with Remus in the rebellion which he had raised within.

The revolt was successful. A revolt is generally successful against a despot, when the great mass of the population desire his downfall. Amulius made a desperate attempt to stem the torrent, but his hour had come. His palace was stormed, and he was slain. The revolution was complete, and Romulus and Remus were masters of the country.

9

The Founding of Rome

AS soon as the excitement and the agitations which attended the sudden revolution by which Amulius was dethroned were in some measure calmed, and tranquillity was restored, the question of the mode in which the new government should be settled, arose. Numitor considered it best that he should call an assembly of the people and lay the subject before them. There was a very large portion of the populace who yet knew nothing certain in respect to the causes of the extraordinary events that had occurred. The city was filled with strange rumors, in all of which truth and falsehood were inextricably mingled, so that they increased rather than allayed the general curiosity and wonder.

Numitor accordingly convened a general assembly of the inhabitants of Alba, in a public square. The rude and rustic mountaineers and peasants whom Romulus had brought to the city came with the rest. Romulus and Remus themselves did not at first appear. Numitor, when the audience was assembled, came forward to address them. He gave them a recital of all the events connected with the usurpation of Amulius. He told them of the original division which had been made thirty or forty years before, of the kingdom and the estates of his father, between Amulius and himself,—of the plans and intrigues by which Amulius had contrived to possess himself of the kingdom and reduce him, Numitor, into subjection to his sway,—of his causing Egestus, Numitor's son, to be slain in the hunting party, and then compelling his little daughter Rhea to become a vestal virgin in order that she might never be married. He then went on to describe the birth of Romulus and Remus, the anger of Amulius when informed of the event, his cruel treatment of the children and of the mother, and his orders that the babes should be drowned in the Tiber. He gave an account of the manner in which the infants had been put into the little wooden ark, of their floating down the stream, and finally landing on the bank, and of their being rescued, protected and fed, by the wolf and the woodpecker. He closed his speech by saying that the young princes were still alive, and that they were then at hand ready to present themselves before the assembly.

As he said these words, Romulus and Remus came forward, and the vast assembly, after gazing for a moment in silent wonder upon their tall and graceful forms, in which they saw combined athletic strength and vigor with manly beauty, they burst into long and loud acclamations. As soon as the applause had in some measure subsided, Romulus and Remus turned to their grandfather and hailed him king. The people responded to this announcement with new plaudits, and Numitor was universally recognized as the rightful sovereign.

It seems that notwithstanding the personal graces and accomplishments of Romulus and Remus, and their popularity among their fellow foresters, that they and their followers made a somewhat rude and wild appearance in the city, and Numitor was very willing, when the state of things had become somewhat settled, that his rustic auxiliaries should find some occasion for withdrawing from the capital and returning again to their own native fastnesses. Romulus and Remus, however, having now learned that they were entitled to the regal name, naturally felt desirous of possessing a little regal power, and thus desired to remain in the city; while still they had too much consideration for their grandfather to wish to deprive him of the government. After some deliberation a plan was devised which promised to gratify the wishes of all.

The plan was this, namely, that Numitor should set apart a place in his kingdom of Latium where Romulus and Remus might build a city for themselves,—taking with them to the spot the whole horde of their retainers. The place which he designated for this purpose was the spot on the banks of the Tiber where the two children had been landed when floating down the stream. It was a wild and romantic region, and the enterprise of building a city upon it was one exactly suited to engage the attention and occupy the powers of such restless spirits as those who had collected under the young princes' standard. Many of these men, it is true, were shepherds and herdsmen, well disposed in mind, though rude and rough in manners. But then there were many others of a very turbulent and unmanageable character, outlaws, fugitives, and adventurers of every description, who had fled to the woods to escape punishment for former crimes, or seek opportunities for the commission of new deeds of rapine and robbery; and who had seized upon the occasion furnished by the insurrection against Amulius to come forth into the world again. Criminals always flock into armies when armies are raised; for war presents to the wicked and depraved all the charms, with but half the danger, of a life of crime. War is in fact ordinarily only a legal organization of crime.

Romulus and Remus entered into their grandfather's plan with great readiness. Numitor promised to aid them in their enterprise by every means in his power. He was to furnish tools and implements, for excavations and building, and artisans so far as artisans were required, and was also to provide such temporary supplies of provisions and stores as might be required at the outset of the undertaking. He gave permission also to any of his subjects to join Romulus and Remus in their undertaking, and they, in order to increase their numbers as much as possible, sent messengers around to the neighboring country inviting all who were disposed, to come and take part in the building of the new city. This invitation was accepted by great numbers of people, from every rank and station in life.

Of course, however, the greater portion of those who came to join the enterprise, were of a very low grade in respect to moral character. Men of industry, integrity, and moral worth, who possessed kind hearts and warm domestic affections, were generally well and prosperously settled each in his own hamlet or town, and were little inclined to break away from the ties which bound them to friends and society, in order to plunge in such a scene of turmoil and confusion as the building of a new city, under such circumstances, must necessarily be. It was of course generally the discontented, the idle, and the bad, that would hope for benefit from such a change as this enterprise proposed to them. Every restless and desperate spirit, every depraved victim of vice, every fugitive and outlaw would be ready to embark in such a scheme, which was to create certainly a new phase in their relations to society, and thus afford them an opportunity to make a fresh beginning. The enterprise at the same time seemed to offer them, through a new organization and new laws, some prospect of release from responsibility for former crimes. In a word, in preparing to lay the foundations of their city, Romulus and Remus found themselves at the head of a very wild and lawless company.

There were seven distinct hills on the ground which was subsequently included within the limits of Rome. Between and among these hills the river meandered by sweeping and graceful curves, and at one point, near the center of what is now the city, the stream passed very near the foot of one of the elevations called the Palatine Hill. Here was the spot where the wooden ark in which Romulus and Remus had been set adrift, had been thrown up upon the shore. The sides of the hill were steep, and between it and the river there was in one part a deep morass. Romulus thought, on surveying the ground with Remus his brother, that this was the best spot for building the city. They could set apart a sufficient space of level ground around the foot of the hill for the houses—inclosing the whole with a wall—while the top of the hill itself might be fortified to form the citadel. The wall and the steep acclivity of the ground would form a protection on three sides of the inclosure, while the morass alone would be a sufficient defense on the part toward the river. Then Romulus was specially desirous to select this spot as the site, as it was here that he and his brother had been saved from destruction in so wonderful a manner.

Situation of Rome

Remus, however, did not concur in these views. A little farther down the stream there was another elevation called the Aventine Hill which seemed to him more suitable for the site of a town. The sides were less precipitous, and thus were more convenient for building ground. Then the land in the immediate vicinity was better adapted to the purposes which they had in view. In a word, the Aventine Hill was, as Remus thought, for every substantial reason, much the best locality; and as for the fact of their having been washed ashore at the foot of the other hill, it was in his opinion an insignificant circumstance, wholly unworthy of being taken seriously into the account in laying the foundation of a city.

The positions in which Remus and Romulus stood in respect to each other, and the feelings which were naturally awakened in their hearts by the circumstances in which they found themselves placed, were such as did not tend to allay any rising asperity which accident might occasion, but rather to irritate and inflame it. In the first place, they were both ardent, impulsive, and imperious. Each was conscious of his strength, and eager to exercise it. Each wished to command, and was wholly unwilling to obey. While they were in adversity, they clung together for mutual help and protection; but now, when they had come into the enjoyment of prosperity and power, the bands of affection which had bound them together were very much weakened, and were finally sundered. Then there was nothing whatever to mark any superiority of one over the other. If they had been of different ages, the younger could have yielded to the elder, in some degree, without wounding his pride. If one had been more prominent than the other in effecting the revolution by which Amulius was dethroned, or if there had been a native difference of temperament or character to mark a distinction, or if either had been designated by Numitor, or selected by popular choice, for the command,—all might have been well. But there seemed in fact to be between them no grounds of distinction whatever. They were twins, so that neither could claim any advantage of birthright. They were equal in size, strength, activity, and courage. They had been equally bold and efficient in effecting the revolution; and now they seemed equally powerful in respect to the influence which they wielded over the minds of their followers. We have been so long accustomed to consider Romulus the more distinguished personage, through the associations connected with his name, that have arisen from his subsequent career, that it is difficult for us to place him and his brother on that footing of perfect equality which they occupied in the estimation of all who knew them in this part of their history. This equality had caused no difference between them thus far, but now, since the advent of power and prosperity prevented their continuing longer on a level, there necessarily came up for decision the terrible question,—terrible when two such spirits as theirs have it to decide,—which was to yield the palm.

The brothers, therefore, having each expressed his preference in respect to the best place for the city, were equally unwilling to recede from the ground which they had taken. Remus thought that there was no reason why he should yield to Romulus, and Romulus was equally unwilling to give way to Remus. Neither could yield, in fact, without in some sense admitting the superiority of the other. The respective partisans of the two leaders began to take sides, and the dissension threatened to become a serious quarrel. Finally, being not yet quite ready for an open rupture, they concluded to refer the question to Numitor, and to abide by his decision. They expected that he would come and view the ground, and so decide where it was best that the city should be built, and thus terminate the controversy.

But Numitor was too sagacious to hazard the responsibility of deciding between two such equally matched and powerful opponents. He endeavored to soothe and quiet the excited feelings of his grandsons, and finally recommended to them to appeal to augury to decide the question. Augury was a mode of ascertaining the divine will in respect to questions of expediency or duty, by means of certain prognostications and signs. These omens were of various kinds, but perhaps the most common were the appearances observed in watching the flight of birds through the air.

It was agreed between Remus and Romulus, in accordance with the advice of Numitor, that the question at issue between them should be decided in this way. They were to take their stations on the two hills respectively—the Palatine and the Aventine, and watch for vultures. The homes of the vultures of Italy were among the summits of the Appenines, and their function in the complicated economy of animal life, was to watch from the lofty peaks of the mountains, or from the still more aërial and commanding positions which they found in soaring at vast elevations in the air, for the bodies of the dead,—whether of men after a battle, or of sheep, or cattle, or wild beasts of the forests, killed by accident or dying of age,—and when found to remove and devour them; and thus to hasten the return of the lifeless elements to other forms of animal and vegetable life. What the earth, and the rite of burial, effects for man in advanced and cultivated stages of society, the vultures of the Appenines were commissioned to perform for all the animal communities of Italy, in Numitor's time.

To enable the vulture to accomplish the work assigned him, he is endowed with an inconceivable strength of wing, to sustain his flight over the vast distances which he has to traverse, and up to the vast elevations to which he must sometimes soar; and also with some mysterious and extraordinary sense, whether of sight or smell, to enable him readily to find, at any hour, the spot where his presence is required, however remote or however hidden it may be. Guided by this instinct, he flies from time to time with a company of his fellows, from mountain to mountain, or wheels slowly in vast circles over the plains—surveying the whole surface of the ground, and assuredly finding his work;—finding it too equally easily, whether it lie exposed in the open field, or is hidden, no matter how secretly, in forest, thicket, grove or glen.

It was, to certain appearances, indicated in the flight of these birds—such as the number that were seen at a time, the quarter of the heavens in which they appeared, the direction in which they flew, as from left to right or from right to left—that the people of Numitor's day were accustomed to look for omens and auguries. So Romulus and Remus took their stations on the hills which they had severally chosen, each surrounded by a company of his own adherents and friends, and began to watch the skies. It was agreed that the decision of the question between the two hills should be determined by the omens which should appear to the respective observers stationed upon them.

But it happened, unfortunately, that the rules for the interpretation of auguries and omens, were far too indefinite and vague to answer the purpose for which they were now appealed to. The most unequivocal distinctness and directness in giving its responses is a very essential requisite in any tribunal that is called upon as an umpire, to settle disputes;

while the ancient auguries and oracles were always susceptible of a great variety of interpretations. When Remus and Romulus commenced their watch no vultures were to be seen from either hill. They waited till evening, still none appeared. They continued to watch through the night. In the morning a messenger came over from the Palatine hill to Remus on the Aventine, informing him that vultures had appeared to Romulus. Remus did not believe it. At last, however, the birds really came into view; a flock of six were seen by Remus, and afterward one of twelve by Romulus. The observations were then suspended, and the parties came together to confer in respect to the result; but the dispute instead of being settled, was found to be in a worse condition than ever. The point now to be determined was whether six vultures seen first, or twelve seen afterward, were the better omen, that is whether numbers, or simple priority of appearance, should decide the question. In contending in respect to this nice point the brothers became more angry with each other than ever. Their respective partisans took sides in the contest, which resulted finally in an open and violent collision. Romulus and Remus themselves seem to have commenced the affray by attacking one another. Faustulus, their foster-father, who, from having had the care of them from their earliest infancy, felt for them an almost parental affection, rushed between them to prevent them from shedding each other's blood. He was struck down and killed on the spot, by some unknown hand. A brother of Faustulus too, named Plistinus, who had lived near to him, and had known the boys from their infancy, and had often assisted in taking care of them, was killed in the endeavor to aid his brother to appease the tumult.

At length the disturbance was quelled. The result of the conflict was, however, to show that Romulus and his party were the strongest. Romulus accordingly went on to build the walls of the city at the spot which he had first chosen. The lines were marked out, and the excavations were commenced with great ceremony.

In laying out the work, the first thing to be done was to draw the lines of what was called the pomœrium. The pomœrium was a sort of symbolical wall, and was formed simply by turning a furrow with a plow all around the city, at a considerable distance from the real walls, for the purpose, not of establishing lines of defense, but of marking out what were to be the limits of the corporation, so to speak, for legal and ceremonial purposes. Of course, the pomœrium included a much greater space than the real walls, and the people were allowed to build houses anywhere within this outer inclosure, or even without it, though not very near to it. Those who built thus were, of course, not protected in case of an attack and of course they would, in such case, be compelled to abandon their houses, and retreat for safety within the proper walls.

So Romulus proceeded to mark out the pomœrium of the city, employing in the work the ceremonies customary on such occasions. The plow used was made of copper, and for a team to draw it a bullock and a heifer were yoked together. Men appointed for the purpose followed the plow, and carefully turned over the clods toward the wall of the city. This seems to have been considered an essential part of the ceremony. At the places where roads were to pass in toward the gates of the city, the plow was lifted out of the ground and carried over the requisite space, so as to leave the turf at those points unbroken. This was a necessary precaution; for there was a certain consecrating influence that was exerted by this ceremonial plowing which hallowed the ground wherever it passed in a manner that would very seriously interfere with its usefulness as a public road.

The form of the space inclosed by the pomœrium, as Romulus plowed it, was nearly square, and it included not merely the Palatine hill itself, but a considerable portion of level land around it.

Though Romulus thus seemed to have conquered, in the strife with Remus, the difficulty was not yet fully settled. Remus was very little disposed to acquiesce in his brother's assumed superiority over him. He was sullen, morose, and ill at ease, and was inclined to take little part in the proceedings which were going on. Finally an occasion occurred which produced a crisis, and brought the rivalry and enmity of the brothers suddenly and forever to an end. Remus was one day standing by a part of the wall which his brother's workmen were building, and expressing, in various ways, and with great freedom, his opinions of his brother's plans; and finally he began to speak contemptuously of the wall which the workmen were building. Romulus all the time was standing by. At length, in order to enforce what he said about the insufficiency of the work, Remus leaped over a portion of it, saying, "This is the way the enemy will leap over your wall." Hereupon Romulus seized a mattock from the hands of one of the laborers, and struck his brother down to the ground with it, saying, "And this is the way that we will kill them if they do." Remus was killed by the blow.

As soon as the deed was done, Romulus was at once overwhelmed with remorse and horror at the atrocity of the crime which he had been so suddenly led to commit. His anguish was so great for a time that he refused all food, and he could not sleep. He caused the dead body of Remus, and also those of Faustulus and of Plistinus, the brother of Faustulus, to be buried with the most solemn and imposing funeral ceremonies, so as to render all possible honor to their memory; and then, not satisfied with this, he instituted and celebrated certain religious rites, to prevent the ghosts of the deceased from coming back to haunt him. The ghosts, or specters of the dead that came back to haunt and terrify the living were called lemures. Hence the celebration which Romulus ordained was called the Lemuria, and it continued to be annually observed in Rome during the whole period of its subsequent history.

Precisely what the ceremonies were which Romulus performed to appease the spirit of his brother can not now be ascertained, as there was no particular description of them recorded. But the Lemuria, as afterward performed, were frequently described by Roman writers, and they were of a very curious and extraordinary character. The time for the celebration of these rites was in May, the anniversary, as was supposed, of the days in which Romulus originally celebrated them. The Lemurial ceremonies extended through three days, or rather nights, although, for some curious reason or other, they were alternate and not consecutive nights. They were the nights of the ninth, eleventh, and thirteenth of

May. The ceremonies were performed in the night, for the reason that it was in the dark hours that ghosts and goblins were accustomed, as was supposed, to roam about the world to haunt and terrify men.

The ceremonies performed on these occasions are thus described. They commenced at midnight. The father of the family would rise at that hour and go out at the door of the house, making certain gesticulations and signals with his hands, which were supposed to have the effect of keeping the specters away. He then washed his hands three times in pure spring water. Then he filled his mouth with a certain kind of black beans for which ghosts were supposed to have some particular fondness. Being thus provided he would walk along, taking the beans out of his mouth as he walked, and throwing them behind him. The specters were supposed to gather up these beans as he threw them down. He must, however, by no means look round to see them. He then, after speaking certain mysterious and cabalistic words, washed his hands again, and then making a frightful noise by striking brass basins together, he shouted out nine times, "Ghosts of this house begone!" This was supposed effectually to drive the specters away—an opinion which was always abundantly confirmed by the fact; for on looking round after this vociferated adjuration, the man always found that the specters were gone!

When by these ceremonies, or ceremonies such as these, Romulus had appeased the spirit of his brother, and those of the guardians of his childhood, his mind became more composed, and he turned his attention once more toward the building of the city. The party of Remus now, of course, since it was deprived of its head, no longer maintained itself, but was gradually broken up and merged in the general mass. Romulus became the sole leader of the enterprise, and immediately turned his attention to the measures to be adopted for a more complete and effectual organization of the community over which he found himself presiding.

In respect to Remus, it ought perhaps to be added, that after his death a story was circulated in Rome that it was a man named Celer and not Romulus, that killed him. This story has not, however, been generally believed. It has been thought more probable that Romulus himself, or some of his partisans and friends, invented and circulated the story of Celer, in order to screen him in some degree from the reproach of so unnatural a crime as the killing of a brother so near and dear to him as Remus had been;—a brother who had shared his infancy with him, who had slept with him, at the same time, in the arms of his mother, who had floated with him down the Tiber in the same ark, been saved from death by the same miraculous intervention, and through all the years of infancy, childhood, and youth, had been his constant playmate, companion, and friend. The crime was as much more atrocious than any ordinary fratricide, as Remus had been nearer to Romulus than any ordinary brother.

10

Organization

THERE has been a great deal of philosophical discussion, and much debate, among historians and chronologists, in attempting to fix the precise year in which Romulus commenced the building of Rome. The difficulty arises from the fact, that no regular records of public events were made in those ancient days. In modern times such records are very systematically kept,—an express object of them being to preserve and perpetuate a knowledge of the exact truth in respect to the time, and the attendant circumstances, relating to all great transactions. On the other hand, the memory of public events in early periods of the world, was preserved only through tradition; and tradition cares little for the exact and the true. She seeks only for what is entertaining. Her function being simply to give pleasure to successive generations of listeners, by exciting their curiosity and wonder with tales,—which, the more strange and romantic they are, the better they are suited to her purpose —she concerns herself very little with such simple verities as dates and names. The exposure of the twin infants of Rhea, supposing such an event to have actually happened, she remembered well, and repeated the narrative of it—adorning it, doubtless, with many embellishments— from age to age, so that the whole story comes down to modern times in full detail; but as to the time when the event took place, she gave herself no concern. The date would have added nothing to the romance of the story, and thus it was neglected and forgotten.

In subsequent times, however, when regular historical annals began to be recorded, chronologists attempted to reason backward, from events whose periods were known, through various data which they ingeniously obtained from the preceding and less formal narratives, until they obtained the dates of earlier events by a species of calculation. In this way the time for the building of Rome was determined to be about the year 754 before Christ. As to Romulus himself, the tradition is that he was but eighteen or twenty years old when he commenced the building of it. If this is true, his extreme youth goes far to palliate some of the wrongs which he perpetrated—wrongs which would have been far more inexcusable if committed with the deliberate purpose of middle life, than if prompted by the unthinking impulses and passions of eighteen.

A certain Roman philosopher, named Varro, who lived some centuries after the building of the city, conceived of a very ingenious plan for discovering the year in which Romulus was born. It was this. By means of the science of astrology, as practiced in those days, certain learned magicians used to predict what the life and fortunes of any man would be, from the aspects and phases of the planets and other heavenly bodies at the time of his birth. The idea of Varro was to reverse this process in the case of Romulus; that is, to deduce from the known facts of his history what must have been the relative situations of the planets and stars when he came into the world! He accordingly applied to a noted astrologer to work out the problem for him. Given, a history of the incidents and events occurring to the man in his progress through life; required, the exact condition of the skies when the child was born. In other words, the astrologer was to determine what must have been the relative positions of the sun, moon, and stars, at the birth of Romulus, in order to produce a being whose life should exhibit such transactions and events as those which appeared in Romulus's subsequent history. When the astrologer had thus ascertained the condition of the skies at the time in question, the astronomers, as Varro concluded, could easily calculate the month and the year when the combination must have occurred.

Now, it was the custom in those days to reckon by Olympiads, which were periods of four years, the series commencing with a great victory at a foot-race in Greece, won by a man named Corœbus, from which event originated the Olympian games, which were afterward celebrated every four years, and which in subsequent ages became so renowned. The time when Corœbus ran his race, and thus furnished an era for all the subsequent chronologists and historians of his country, is generally regarded as about the year 776 before Christ; and the result of the calculations of Varro's astrologer, and of the astronomers who perfected it, was, that to lead such a life as Romulus led, a man must have been born at a time corresponding with the first year of the second Olympiad; that is, taking off from 776, four years, for the first Olympiad, the first year of the second Olympiad would be 772; this would make the time of his birth 772 before Christ; and then deducting eighteen years more, for the age of Romulus when he began to build his wall, we have 754 before Christ as the era of the foundation of Rome. This method of determining a point in chronology seems so absurd, according to the ideas of the present day, that we can hardly resist the conclusion, that Varro, in making his investigation, was really guided by other and more satisfactory modes of determining the point, and that the horoscope was not what he actually relied upon. However this may be, the era which he fixed upon has been very generally received, though many others have been proposed by the different learned men who have successively investigated the question.

According to the accounts given by the early writers, the constructions which Romulus and his companions made were of a very rude and simple character; such as might have been expected from a company of boys: for boys we ought perhaps to consider them all, since it is not to be presumed that the troop, in respect to age and experience, would be much in advance of the leaders. The wall which they built about the city was probably only a substantial stone fence, and their houses were huts and hovels. Even the palace, for there was a building erected for Romulus himself which was called the palace, was made, it is said, of rushes. Perhaps the meaning is that it was thatched with rushes,—or possibly the expression refers to a mode of building sometimes adopted in the earlier stages of civilization, in which straw, or rushes, or some similar material is mixed with mud or clay to help bind the mass together, the whole being afterward dried in the sun. Walls thus made have been found to possess much more strength and durability than would be supposed possible for such a material to attain.

However this may be, the hamlet of huts which Romulus and his wild coadjutors built and walled in, must have appeared at the time, to all observers, a very rude and imperfect attempt at building a city; in fact it must have seemed to them, if it is true that Romulus was at that time only eighteen years old, more like a frolic of thoughtless boys than a serious enterprise of men. Romulus, however, whatever others may have thought of his work, was wholly in earnest. He felt that he was a prince, and proud of his birth, and fully conscious of his intellectual and personal power, he determined that he would have a kingdom.

It seems, however, that thus far he had not been considered as possessing any thing like regal authority over his company of followers, but had been regarded only as a sort of chieftain exercising an undefined and temporary power; for as soon as the huts were built and the inclosures made, he is said to have convened an assembly of the people, for consultation in respect to the plan of government that they should form. Romulus introduced the business of this meeting by a speech appropriate to the occasion, which speech is reported by an ancient historian somewhat as follows. Whether Romulus actually spoke the words thus attributed to him, or whether the report contains only what the reporter himself imagined him to say, there is now no means of knowing.

"We have now," said Romulus, according to this record, "completed the building of our city, so far as at present we are able to do it; and it must be confessed that if we were required to depend for protection against a serious attack from an enemy, on the height of our walls, or on their strength and solidity, our prospects would not be very encouraging. But our walls we must remember are not what we rely upon. No walls can be so high, that an enemy can not scale them. The dependence must be after all on the men within the city, and not on the ramparts and entrenchments which surround it, whatever those ramparts and entrenchments may be. We must therefore rely upon ourselves, for our safety—upon our valor, our discipline, our union and harmony. It is courage and energy in the people, not strength in outward defenses, on which the safety and prosperity of a State must depend.

"The great work before us therefore is yet to be done. We have to organize a government under which order and discipline may come in, to control and direct our energies, and prepare us to meet whatever future exigencies may arise, whether of peace or war. What form shall be given to this government is the question that you have now to consider. I have learned by inquiry that there are various modes of government adopted among men, and between these we have now to decide. Shall our commonwealth be governed by one man? Or shall we select a certain number of the wisest and bravest of the citizens, and commit the administration of public affairs to them? Or, in the third place, shall we commit the management of the government to the control of the people at large? Each of these three forms has its advantages, and each is attended with its own peculiar dangers. You are to choose between them. Only when the decision is once made, let us all unite in maintaining the government which shall be established, whatever its form may be."

The result of the deliberation which followed, after the delivery of this address, was that the government of the state should be, like the government of Alba, under which the followers of Romulus had been born, a monarchy; and that Romulus himself should be king. He was a prince by birth, an inheritor of regal rank and power, by regular succession, from a line of kings. He had shown himself, too, by his deeds, to be worthy of power. He was courageous, energetic, sagacious, and universally esteemed. It was decided accordingly that he should be king, and he was proclaimed such by all the assembled multitude, with long and loud acclamations.

Notwithstanding the apparent unanimity and earnestness of the people, however, in calling Romulus to the throne, he evinced, as the story goes, the proper degree of that reluctance and hesitation which a suitable regard to appearances seems in all ages to require of public men when urged to accept of power. He was thankful to the people for the marks of their confidence, but he could not consent to assume the responsibilities and prerogatives of power until the choice made by his countrymen had been confirmed by the divinities of the land. So he resolved on instituting certain solemn religious ceremonies, during the progress of which he hoped to receive some manifestation of the divine will. These ceremonies consisted principally of sacrifices which he caused to be offered on the plain near the city. While Romulus was engaged in these services, the expected token of the divine approval appeared in a supernatural light which shone upon his hand. At least it was said that such a light was seen, and the appearing of it was considered as clearly confirming the right of Romulus to the throne. He no longer made any objection to assuming the government of the new city as its acknowledged king.

The first object to which he gave his attention was the organization of the people, and the framing of the general constitution of society. The community over which he was called to preside had consisted thus far of very heterogeneous and discordant materials. Vast numbers of the people were of the humblest and most degraded condition, consisting of ignorant peasants, some stupid, others turbulent and ungovernable; and of refugees from justice, such as thieves, robbers, and outlaws of every degree. But then, on the other hand, there were many persons of standing and respectability. The sons of families of wealth and influence in Alba had, in many cases, joined the expedition, and at last, when the building of the city had advanced so far as to make it appear that the enterprise might succeed, more men of age and character came to join it, so that Romulus found himself, when he formally assumed the kingly power, at the head of a community which contained the elements of a very respectable commonwealth. These elements were, however, thus far all mingled together in complete confusion, and the work that was first to be done was to adopt some plan for classifying and arranging them.

It is most probable, as a matter of fact, that the organization and the institutions which in subsequent times appeared in the Roman state, were not deliberately planned and formally introduced by Romulus at the outset, but that they gradually grew up in the progress of time, and that afterward historians and philosophers, in speculating upon them at their leisure, carried back the history of them to the earliest times, in order, by so doing, to honor the founder of the city, and also to exalt and aggrandize the institutions themselves in public estimation, by celebrating the antiquity and dignity of their origin.

The institutions which Romulus actually founded, were of a very republican character, if the accounts of subsequent writers are to be believed. He established, it is true, a gradation of ranks, but the most important offices, civil and military, were filled, it is said, by election on the part of the people. In the first place, the whole population was divided into three portions, which were called tribes, which word was formed from the Latin word tres, meaning three. These tribes chose each three presiding officers, selecting for the purpose the oldest and most distinguished of their number. It is probable, in fact, that Romulus himself really made the selection, and that the action of the people was confined to some sort of expression of assent and concurrence for it is difficult to imagine how any other kind of election than this could be possible among so rude and ignorant a multitude. The tribes were then subdivided each into thirty counts or counties, and each of these likewise elected its head. Thus there was a large body of magistrates or chieftains appointed, ninety-nine in number, namely, nine heads of tribes and ninety heads of counties. Romulus himself added one to the number, of his own independent selection, which made the hundredth. The men thus chosen, constituted what was called the senate. They formed the great legislative council of the nation. They and the families descending from them became, in subsequent times, an aristocratic and privileged class, called the Patricians. The remaining portion of the population were called Plebeians.

The Plebeians comprised, of course, the industrial and useful classes, and were in rank and station inferior to the Patricians. They were, however, not all upon a level with each other, for they were divided into two great classes, called patrons and clients. The patrons were the employers, the proprietors, the men of influence and capital. The clients were the employed, the dependent, the poor. The clients were to perform services of various kinds for the patrons, and the patrons were to reward, to protect, and to defend the clients. All these arrangements Romulus is said to have ordained by his enactments, and thus introduced as elements in the social constitution of the state. It is more probable, however, that instead of being thus expressly established, by the authority of Romulus as a lawgiver, they gradually grew up of themselves, perhaps with some fostering attention and care on his part, and possibly under some positive regulation of law. For such important and complicated relations as these are not of a nature to be easily called into existence and action, in an extended and unorganized community, by the mere fiat of a military chieftain.

Perhaps, however, it is not intended by the ancient historians, in referring all these complicated arrangements of the Roman civil polity to the enactments of Romulus, to convey the idea that he introduced them at once in all their completeness, at the outset of his reign. Romulus continued king of Rome for nearly forty years, and instead of making formal and positive enactments, he may have gradually introduced the arrangements ascribed to him, as usages which he fostered and encouraged,—confirming and sanctioning them from time to time, when occasion required, by edicts and laws.

However this may have been, it is certain that Romulus, in the course of his reign, laid the foundation of the future greatness and glory of Rome, by the energy with which he acted in introducing order, system, and discipline into the community which he found gathered around him. He seems to have had the sagacity to perceive from the outset that the great evil and danger which he had to fear was the prevalence of the spirit of disorder and misrule among his followers. In fact, nothing but tumult and confusion was to have been expected from such a lawless horde as his, and even after the city was built, the presumption must have been very strong in the mind of any considerate and prudent man, against the possibility of ever regulating and controlling such a mass of heterogeneous and discordant materials, by any human means. Romulus saw, however, that in effecting this purpose lay the only hope of the success of his enterprise, and he devoted himself with great assiduity and care, and at the same time with great energy and success, to the work of organizing it. The great leading objects of his life, from the time that he commenced the government of the new city, were to arrange and regulate social institutions, to establish laws, to introduce discipline, to teach and accustom men to submit to authority, and to bring in the requirements of law, and the authority of the various recognized relations of social life, to control and restrain the wayward impulses of the natural heart.

As a part of this system of policy, he laid great stress upon the parental and family relation. He saw in the tie which binds the father to the child and the child to the father, a natural bond which he foresaw would greatly aid him in keeping the turbulent and boisterous propensities of human nature under some proper control. He accordingly magnified and confirmed the natural force of parental authority by adding the sanctions of law to it. He defined and established the power of the father to govern and control the son, rightly considering that the father is the natural ally of the state in restraining young men from violence, and enforcing habits of industry and order upon them, at an age when they most need control. He clothed parents, therefore, with authority to fulfill this function, considering that what he thus aided them to do, was so much saved for the civil magistrate and the state. In fact, he carried this so far that it is said that the dependence of the child upon the father, under the institutions of Romulus, was more complete, and was protracted to a later period than was the case under the laws of any other nation. The power of the father over his household was supreme. He was a magistrate, so far as his children were concerned, and could thus not only require their services, and inflict light punishments for disobedience upon them, as with us, but he could sentence them to the severest penalties of the law, if guilty of crime.

The laws were equally stringent in respect to the marriage tie. Death was the penalty for the violation of the marriage vows. All property belonging to the husband and to the wife was held by them in common, and the wife, if she survived the husband, and if the husband died without a will, became his sole heir. In a word, the laws of Romulus evince a very strong desire on the part of the legislator to sustain the sacredness and to magnify the importance of the family tie; and to avail himself of those instinctive principles of obligation and duty which so readily arise in the human mind out of the various relations of the family state, in the plans which he formed for subduing the impulses and regulating the action of his rude community.

He devoted great attention too to the institutions of religion. He knew well that such lawless and impetuous spirits as his could never be fully subdued and held in proper subordination to the rules of social order and moral duty, without the influence of motives drawn from the spiritual world; and he accordingly adopted vigorous measures for confirming and perpetuating such religious observances as were at that time observed, and in introducing others. Every public act which he performed was always accompanied and sanctioned by religious solemnities. The rites and ceremonies which he instituted seem puerile to us, but they were full of meaning and of efficacy in the view of those who performed them. There was, for example, a class of religious functionaries called augurs, whose office it was to interpret the divine will by means of certain curious indications which it was their special profession to understand. There were three of these augurs, and they were employed on all public occasions, both in peace and war, to ascertain from the omens whether the enterprise or the work in regard to which they were consulted was or was not favored by the councils of heaven. If the augury was propitious the work was entered upon with vigor and confidence. If otherwise, it was postponed or abandoned.

The omens which the augurs observed were of various kinds, being drawn sometimes from certain peculiarities in the form and structure of the internal organs of animals offered in sacrifice, sometimes from the appearance of birds in the sky, their numbers or the direction of their flight, and sometimes from the forms of clouds, the appearance of the lightning, and the sound of the thunder. Whenever the augurs were to take the auspices from any of the signs of the sky, the process was this. They would go with solemn ceremony to some high place—in Rome there was a station expressly consecrated to this purpose on the Capitoline hill,—and there, with a sort of magical wand which they had for the purpose, one of the number would determine and indicate the four quarters of the heaven, pointing out in a solemn manner the directions of east, west, north and south. The augur would then take his stand with his back to the west and his face of course to the east. The north would then be on his left hand and the south at his right. He would then, in this position watch for the signs. If it was from the thunder that the auspices were to be taken, the augur would listen to hear from what quarter of the heavens it came. If the lightning appeared in the east and the sound of the thunder seemed to come from the northward, the presage was favorable. So it was if the chain of lightning seen in the sky appeared to pass from cloud to cloud above, instead of descending to the ground. On the other hand, thunder sounding as if it came from the southward, and lightning striking down to the earth, were both unpropitious omens. As to birds, some were of good omen, as vultures, eagles and woodpeckers. Others were evil, as ravens and owls. Various inferences were drawn too from the manner in which the birds that appeared in the air, were seen to fly, and from the sound of their note at the time when the observation was made.

By these and many similar means the government of Romulus vainly endeavored to ascertain the will of heaven in respect to the plans and enterprises in which they were called upon from time to time to engage. There was perhaps in these observances much imposture, and much folly; still they could only have been sustained, in their influence and ascendency over the minds of the people, by a sincere veneration on their part for some unseen and spiritual power, and a reverent desire to conform the public measures of their government to what they supposed to be the divine will.

By such measures as we have thus described Romulus soon produced order out of confusion within his little commonwealth. The enterprise which he had undertaken and the great success which had thus far followed it, attracted great attention, and he soon found that great numbers began to come in from all the surrounding country to join him. Many of these were persons of still worse character than those who had adhered to him at first, and he soon found that to admit them indiscriminately into the city would be to endanger the process of organization which was now so well begun. He accordingly set apart a hill near to his city called the Capitoline hill, as an asylum for them, where they could remain in safety under regulations suitable to their condition, and without interfering with the arrangements which he had made for the rest. This asylum soon became a very attractive place for all the vagabonds, outlaws, thieves and robbers of the country. Romulus welcomed them all, and as fast as they came he busied himself with plans to furnish them with employment and subsistence. He enlisted some of them in his army. Some he employed to cultivate the ground in the territory belonging to the city. Others were engaged as servants for the people within the walls—being taken into the city, in small numbers, from time to time, as fast as they could be safely received. In process of time, however, the walls of the city were extended so as to include the Capitoline hill, and thus at last the whole mass was brought into Rome together.

11

Wives

EVERY reader who has made even the smallest beginning in the study of ancient history, must be acquainted, in general, with the mode which Romulus adopted to provide the people of his city with wives, by the transaction which is commonly called in history the rape of the Sabines. The deed itself, as it actually occurred, may perhaps have been one of great rudeness, violence, and cruelty. If so, the historians who described it contrived to soften the character of it, and to divest it in a great measure of the repulsive features which might have been supposed to characterize such a transaction, for, according to the narrative which they give us, the whole proceeding was conducted in such a manner as to evince not only great ingenuity and sagacity on the part of Romulus and his government, but also great moderation and humanity. The circumstances, as the historians relate them, were these:

As might naturally be supposed from the manner in which the company which formed the population of Rome had been collected, it consisted at first almost wholly of men. The laws and regulations referred to in the last chapter, in respect to the family relation, were those framed after the organization of the community had become somewhat advanced, since at the outset there could be very few families, inasmuch as the company which first met together to build the city, consisted simply of an army of young men. It is true that among those who joined them at first there were some men of middle life and some families,—

still, as is always the case with new cities and countries suddenly and rapidly settled, the population consisted almost entirely of men.

It was necessary that the men should have wives. There were several reasons for this. First, it was necessary for the comfort and happiness of the people themselves. A community of mere men is gloomy and desolate. Secondly, for the continuance and perpetuity of the state it was necessary that there should be wives and children, so that when one generation should have passed away there might be another to succeed it. And, thirdly, for the preservation of order and law. Men unmarried are, in the mass, proverbially ungovernable. Nothing is so effectual in keeping a citizen away from scenes of tumult and riot as a wife and children at home. The fearful violence of the riots and insurrections of which the city of Paris has so often been the scene, is explained, in a great degree, by the circumstance that so immense a proportion of the population are unmarried. They have no homes, and no defenseless wives and children to fear for, and so they fear nothing, but give themselves up, in times of public excitement, to the wildest impulses of passion. Romulus seems to have understood this, and his first care was to provide the way by which as many as possible of his people should be married.

The first measure which he adopted, was to send ambassadors around to the neighboring states, soliciting alliances with them, and stipulations allowing of intermarriages between his people and theirs. The proposal seemed not unreasonable, and it was made in an unassuming and respectful manner. In the message which Romulus commissioned the ambassadors to deliver, he admitted that his colony was yet small, and by no means equal in influence and power to the kingdoms whose alliance he desired; but he reminded those whom he addressed that great results came sometimes in the end from very inconsiderable beginnings, and that their enterprise thus far, though yet in its infancy, had been greatly prospered, and was plainly an object of divine favor, and that the time might not be far distant when the new state would be able fully to reciprocate such favors as it might now receive.

The neighboring kings to whom these embassies were sent rejected the proposals with derision. They did not even give serious answers, obviously considering the new city as a mere temporary gathering and encampment of adventurers and outlaws, which would be as transient as it was rude and irregular. They looked to see it break up as suddenly and tumultuously as it had been formed. They accordingly sent back word to Romulus that he must resort to the same plan to get women for his city that he had adopted to procure recruits of men. He must open an asylum for them. The low and the dissolute would come flocking to him then, they said, from all parts, and vagabond women would make just the kind of wives for vagabond men.

Of course, the young men of the city were aroused to an extreme pitch of indignation at receiving this response. They were clamorous for war. They wished Romulus to lead them out against some of these cities at once, and allow them at the same time to revenge the insults which they had received, and to provide themselves with wives by violence, since they could not obtain them by solicitation. But Romulus restrained their ardor, saying that they must do nothing rashly, and promising to devise a better way than theirs to attain the end.

The plan which he devised was to invite the people of the surrounding states and cities both men and women, to come to Rome, with a view of seizing some favorable occasion for capturing the women while they were there, and driving the men away. The difficulty in the way of the execution of this plan was obviously to induce the people to come, and especially to bring the young women with them. The native timidity of the maidens, joined to the contemptuous feelings which their fathers and brothers cherished, in regard to every thing pertaining to the new city, would very naturally keep them away, unless something could be devised which would exert a very strong attraction.

Romulus waited a little time, in order that any slight excitement which had been produced by his embassy should have had time to subside, and then he made, or pretended to make, a great discovery in a field not far from his town. This discovery was the finding of an ancient altar of Neptune, under ground. The altar was brought to view by some workmen who were making excavations at the place. How it came to be under ground, and who had built it, no one knew. The rumor of this great discovery was spread immediately in every direction. Romulus attached great importance to the event. The altar had undoubtedly been built, he thought, by the ancient inhabitants of the country, and the finding it was a very momentous occurrence. It was proper that the occasion should be solemnized by suitable religious observances.

Accordingly, arrangements were made for a grand celebration. In addition to the religious rites, Romulus proposed that a great fair should be held on a plain near the city at the same time. Booths were erected, and the merchants of all the neighboring cities were invited to come, bringing with them such articles as they had for sale, and those who wished to buy were to come with their money. In a word, arrangements were made for a great and splendid festival.

There were to be games too, races, and wrestlings, and other athletic sports, such as were in vogue in those times. The celebration was to continue for many days, and the games and sports were to come at the end. Romulus sent messengers to all the surrounding country to proclaim the programme of these entertainments, and to invite every body to come; and he adroitly arranged the details in such a manner that the chief attractions for grave, sober-minded and substantial men should be on the earlier days of the show, and that the latter days should be devoted to lighter amusements, such as would possess a charm for the young, the light-hearted and the happy. It was among this last class that he naturally expected to find the maidens whom his men would choose in looking for wives.

When the time arrived the spectacles commenced. There was a great concourse at the outset, but the people who first came, were, as Romulus supposed would be the case, chiefly men. They came in companies, as if for mutual support and protection, and they exhibited in a greater or less degree an air of suspicion, watchfulness and mistrust. They were, however, received with great cordiality and kindness. They were conducted about the town, and were astonished to find how considerable a town it was. The streets, the houses, the walls, the temples, simple in construction as they were, far surpassed the expectations they had formed. The visitors were treated with great hospitality, and entertained in a manner which, considering the circumstances of the case, was quite sumptuous. The women and children too, who came on these first days, received from all the Romans very special attention and regard.

As the celebrations went on from day to day, a considerable change took place in the character and appearance of the company. The men ceased to be suspicious and watchful. Some went home, and carried such reports of the new city, and of the kindness, and hospitality, and gentle behavior of the inhabitants, that new visitors came continually to see for themselves. Every day the proportion of stern and suspicious men diminished, and that of gay and happy-looking youths and maidens increased.

In the mean time, the men of the city were under strict injunctions from Romulus to treat their guests in the most respectful manner, leaving them entirely at liberty to go and come as they pleased, except so far as they could detain them by treating them with kindness and attention, and devising new sports and amusements for them from day to day. Things continued in this state for two or three weeks, during all which time the new city was a general place of resort for the people of all the surrounding country. Of course a great many agreeable acquaintances would naturally be formed between the young men of the city and their visitors, as accidental circumstances, or individual choice and preference brought them together; and thus, without any directions on the subject from Romulus, each man would very naturally occupy himself, in anticipation of the general seizure which he knew was coming, in making his selection beforehand, of the maiden whom he intended, when the time for the seizure came, to make his own; and the maiden herself would probably be less terrified, and make less resistance to the attempt to capture her, than if it were by a perfect stranger that she was to be seized.

All this Romulus seems very adroitly to have arranged. The time for the final execution of the scheme was to be the last day of the celebration. The best spectacle and show of all was to take place on that day. The Romans were directed to come armed to this show, but to keep their arms carefully concealed beneath their garments. They were to do nothing till Romulus gave the signal. He was himself to be seated upon a sort of throne, in a conspicuous place, where all could see him, presiding, as it were, over the assembly, while the spectacle went on; and finally, when he judged that the proper moment had arrived, he was to give the signal by taking off a certain loose article of dress which he wore—a sort of cloak or mantle—and folding it up, and then immediately unfolding it again. This mantle was a sort of badge of royalty, and was gayly adorned with purple stripes upon a white ground. It was well adapted, therefore, to the purpose of being used as a signal, inasmuch as any motions that were made with it could be very easily seen.

Every thing being thus arranged, the assembly was convened, and the games and spectacles went on. The Romans were full of excitement and trepidation, each one having taken his place as near as possible to the maiden whom he was intending to seize, and occupying himself with keeping his eye upon her as closely as he could, without seeming to do so, and at the same time watching the royal mantle, and every movement made by the wearer of it, that he might catch the signal the instant that it should be made. All this time the men among the guests at the entertainment were off their guard, and wholly at their ease—having no suspicion whatever of the mine that was ready to be sprung beneath them. The wives, mothers, and children, too, were all safe, as well as unsuspicious of danger; for Romulus had given special charge that no married woman should be molested. The men had had ample time and opportunity in the many days of active social intercourse which they had enjoyed with their guests, to know who were free, and they were forbidden in any instance to take a wife away from her husband.

At length the moment arrived for giving the signal. Romulus took off his mantle, folded it, and then unfolded it again. The Romans immediately drew their swords, and rushed forward, each to secure his own prize. A scene of the greatest excitement and confusion ensued. The whole company of visitors perceived of course that some great act of treachery was perpetrated upon them, but they were wholly in the dark in respect to the nature and design of it. They were chiefly unarmed, and wholly unprepared for so sudden an attack, and they fled in all directions in dismay, protecting themselves and their wives and children as well as they could, as they retired, and aiming only to withdraw as large a number as possible from the scene of violence and confusion that prevailed. The Romans were careful not to do them any injury, but, on the contrary, to allow them to withdraw, and to take away all the mothers and children without any molestation. In fact, it was the very object and design of the onset which they made upon the company, not only to seize upon the maidens, but to drive all the rest of their visitors away. The men, therefore, in the excitement and terror of the moment, fled in all directions, taking with them those whom they could most readily secure, who were, of course, those whom the Romans left to them; while the Romans themselves withdrew with their prizes, and secured them within the walls of the city.

In reading this extraordinary story, we naturally feel a strong disposition to inquire what part the damsels themselves took, when they found themselves thus suddenly seized and carried away, by these daring and athletic assailants. Did they resist and struggle to get free, or did they yield themselves without much opposition to their fate? That they did not resist effectually is plain, for the Roman young men succeeded in carrying them away, and securing them. It may be that they attempted to resist, but found their strength overpowered by the desperate and reckless violence of their captors. And yet, it can not be denied that woman is endued with the power of making by various means a very formidable opposition to any attempt to abduct her by any single man, when she is thoroughly in earnest about it. How it was in fact in this case we have no direct information, and we have consequently no means of forming any opinion in respect to the light in which this rough and lawless mode of wooing was regarded by the objects of it, except from the events which subsequently occurred.

One incident took place while the Romans were seizing and carrying away their prizes, which was afterward long remembered, as it became the foundation of a custom which continued for many centuries to form a part of the marriage ceremony at Rome. It seems that some young men—very young, and of a humble class—had seized a peculiarly beautiful girl—one of some note and consideration, too, among her countrywomen—and were carrying her away, like the rest. Some other young Romans of the patrician order seeing this, and thinking that so beautiful a maiden ought not to fall to the share of such plebeians, immediately set out in full pursuit to rescue her. The plebeians hurried along to escape from them, calling out at the same time, "Thalassio! Thalassio!" which means "For Thalassius, For Thalassius." They meant by this to convey the idea that the prize which they had in possession was intended not for any one of their own number, but for Thalassius. Now Thalassius was a young noble universally known and very highly esteemed by all his countrymen, and when the rescuing party were thus led to suppose that the beautiful lady was intended for him, they acquiesced immediately, and desisted from their attempt to recapture her, and thus by the aid of their stratagem the plebeians carried off their prize in safety. When this circumstance came afterward to be known, the ingenuity of the young plebeians, and the success of their manœuver, excited very general applause, and the exclamation, Thalassio, passed into a sort of proverb, and was subsequently adopted as an exclamation of assent and congratulation, to be used by the spectators at a marriage ceremony.

Romulus had issued most express and positive orders that the young captives should be treated after their seizure in the kindest and most respectful manner, and should be subject to no violence, and no ill-treatment of any kind, other than that necessary for conveying them to the places of security previously designated. They suffered undoubtedly a greater or less degree of distress and terror,—but finding that they were treated, after their seizure, with respectful consideration, and that they were left unmolested by their captors, they gradually recovered their composure during the night, and in the morning were quite self-possessed and calm. Their fathers and brothers in the mean time had gone home to their respective cities, taking with them the women and children that they had saved, and burning with indignation and rage against the perpetrators of such an act of treachery as had been practiced upon them. They were of course in a state of great uncertainty and suspense in respect to the fate which awaited the captives, and were soon eagerly engaged in forming and discussing all possible plans for rescuing and recovering them. Thus the night was passed in agitation and excitement, both within and without the city,—the excitement of terror and distress, great perhaps, though subsiding on the part of the captives, and of resentment and rage which grew deeper and more extended every hour, on the part of their countrymen.

When the morning came, Romulus ordered the captive maidens to be all brought together before him in order that he might make as it were an apology to them for the violence to which they had been subjected, and explain to them the circumstances which had impelled the Romans to resort to it.

"You ought not," said he, "to look upon it as an indignity that you have been thus seized, for the object of the Romans in seizing you was not to dishonor you, or to do you any injury, but only to secure you for their wives in honorable marriage; and far from being displeased with the extraordinariness of the measures which they have adopted to secure you, you ought to take pride in them, as evincing the ardor and strength of the affection with which you have inspired your lovers. I will assure you that when you have become their wives you shall be treated with all the respect and tenderness that you have been accustomed to experience under your fathers' roofs. The brief coercion which we have employed for the purpose of securing you in the first instance,—a coercion which we were compelled to resort to by the necessity of the case,—is the only rudeness to which you will ever be exposed. Forgive us then for this one liberty which we have taken, and consider that the fault, whatever fault in it there may be, is not ours, but that of your fathers and brothers who rejected our offers for voluntary and peaceful alliances, and thus compelled us to resort to this stratagem or else to lose you altogether. Your destiny if you unite with us will be great and glorious. We have not taken you captive to make you prisoners or slaves, or to degrade you in any way from your former position; but to exalt you to positions of high consideration in a new and rising colony;—a colony which is surely destined to become great and powerful, and of which we mean you to be the chief glory and charm."

The young and handsome Romans stood by while Romulus made this speech, their countenances animated with excitement and pleasure. The maidens themselves seemed much inclined to yield to their fate. Their resentment gradually subsided. It has been, in fact, in all ages, characteristic of women to be easily led to excuse and forgive any wrong on the part of another which is prompted by love for herself: and these injured maidens seemed gradually to come to the conclusion, that considering all the circumstances of the case their abductors were not so much in fault after all. In a short time an excellent understanding was established, and they were all married. There were, it is said, about five or six hundred of them, and it proved that most of them were from the nation of the Sabines, a nation which inhabited a territory north of the colony of the Romans. The capital of the Sabines was a city called Cures. Cures was about twenty miles from Rome.

The Sabines, in deliberating on the course which they should pursue in the emergency, found themselves in a situation of great perplexity. In the first place the impulse which urged them to immediate acts of retaliation and hostility was restrained by the fact that so many of their beloved daughters were wholly in the power of their enemies, and they could not tell what cruel fate might await the captives if they were themselves to resort to any measures that would exasperate or provoke the captors. Then again their own territory was very much exposed and they were by no means certain, in case a war should be commenced between them and the Romans, how it would end. Their own population was much divided, being scattered over the territory, or settled in various cities and towns which were but slightly fortified, and consequently were much exposed to assault in case the Romans were to make an incursion into their country. In view of all these considerations the Sabines concluded that it would be best for them on the whole, to try the influence of gentle measures, before resorting to open war.

They therefore sent an embassy to Romulus, to remonstrate in strong terms against the wrong which the Romans had done them by their treacherous violence, and to demand that the young women should be restored. "If you will restore them to us now," said they, "we will overlook the affront which you have put upon us, and make peace with you; and we will enter into an alliance with you so that hereafter your people and ours may be at liberty to intermarry in a fair and honorable way, but we can not submit to have our daughters taken away from us by treachery and force."

Reasonable as this proposition seems, Romulus did not think it best to accede to it. It was, in fact, too late, for such deeds once done can hardly be undone. Romulus replied, that the women, being now the wives of the Romans, could not be surrendered. The violence, he said, of which the Sabines complained was unavoidable. No other possible way had been open to them for gaining the end. He was willing, he added, to enter into a treaty of peace and alliance with the Sabines, but they must acknowledge, as a preliminary to such a treaty, the validity of the marriages, which, as they had already been consummated, could not now be annulled.

The Sabines, on their part, could not accede to these proposals. Being, however, still reluctant to commence hostilities, they continued the negotiations—though while engaged in them they seemed to anticipate an unfavorable issue, for they were occupied all the time in organizing troops, strengthening the defenses of their villages and towns, and making other vigorous preparations for war.

The Romans, in the mean time, seemed to find the young wives which they had procured by these transactions a great acquisition to their colony. It proved, too, that they not only prized the acquisition, but they exulted so much in the ingenuity and success of the stratagem by which their object had been effected, that a sort of symbolical violence in taking the bride became afterward a part of the marriage ceremony in all subsequent weddings. For always, in future years, when the new-married wife was brought home to her husband's house, it was the custom for him to take her up in his arms at the door, and carry her over the threshold as if by force, thus commemorating by this ceremony the coercion which had signalized the original marriages of his ancestors, the founders of Rome.

12

The Sabine War

WHILE the negotiations with the Sabines were still pending, Romulus became involved in another difficulty, which for a time assumed a very threatening aspect. This difficulty was a war which broke out, somewhat suddenly, in consequence of the invasion of the Roman territories by a neighboring chieftain named Acron. Acron was the sovereign of a small state, whose capital was a town called Cænina. This Cænina is supposed to have been only four or five miles distant from Romulus's city,—a fact which shows very clearly on how small a scale the deeds and exploits connected with the first foundation of the great empire, which afterward became so extended and so renowned, were originally performed, and how intrinsically insignificant they were, in themselves, though momentous in the extreme in respect to the consequences that flowed from them.

Acron was a bold, energetic, and determined man, who had already acquired great fame by his warlike exploits, and who had long been watching the progress of the new colony with an evil eye. He thought that if it were allowed to take root, and to grow, it might, at some future day, become a formidable enemy, both to him, and also to the other states in that part of Italy. He had been very desirous, therefore, of finding some pretext for attacking the new city, and when he heard of the seizure of the Sabine women, he thought that the time had arrived. He, therefore, urged the Sabines to make war at once upon the

Romans, and promised, if they would do so, to assist them with all the forces that he could command. The Sabines, however, were so unwilling to proceed to extremities, and spent so much time in negotiations and embassies, that Acron's patience was at length wholly exhausted by the delays, and he resolved to undertake the extermination of the new colony himself alone.

So he gathered together a rude and half-organized army, and advanced toward Rome. Romulus, who had been informed of his plans and preparations, went out to meet him. The two armies came in view of each other on an open plain, not far from the city. Romulus advanced at the head of his troops, while Acron appeared likewise in the forefront of the invaders. After uttering in the hearing of each other, and of the assembled armies, various exclamations of challenge and defiance, it was at length agreed that the question at issue should be decided by single combat, the two commanders themselves to be the champions. Romulus and Acron accordingly advanced into the middle of the field, while their armies drew up around them, forming a sort of ring within which the combatants were to engage.

The interest which would be naturally felt by such an encounter, was increased very much by the strong contrast that was observed in the appearance of the warriors. Romulus was very young, and though tall and athletic in form, his countenance exhibited still the expression of softness and delicacy characteristic of youth. Acron, on the other hand, was a war-worn veteran, rugged, hardy, and stern; and the throngs of martial spectators that surrounded the field, when they saw the combatants as they came forward to engage, anticipated a very unequal contest. Romulus was nevertheless victorious. As he went into the battle, he made a vow to Jupiter, that if he conquered his foe, he would ascribe to the god all the glory of the victory, and he would set up the arms and spoils of Acron at Rome, as a trophy sacred to Jupiter, in honor of the divine aid through which the conquest should be achieved. It was in consequence of this vow, as the old historians say, that Romulus prevailed in the combat. At all events, he did prevail. Acron was slain, and while Romulus was stripping the fallen body of its armor on the field, his men were pursuing the army of Acron, for the soldiers fled in dismay toward their city, as soon as they saw that the single combat had gone against their king.

Cænina was not in a condition to make any defense, and it was readily taken. When the city was thus in the power of Romulus, he called the inhabitants together, and said to them, that he cherished no hostile or resentful feelings toward them. On the contrary, he wished to have them his allies and friends, and he promised them, that if they would abandon Cænina, and go with him to Rome, they should all be received as brothers, and be at once incorporated into the Roman state, and admitted to all the privileges of citizens. The people of Cænina, when the first feelings of terror and distress which their falling into the power of their enemies naturally awakened, had been in some measure allayed, readily acquiesced in this arrangement, and were all transferred to Rome. Their coming made a great addition not only to the population and strength of the city, but vastly increased the celebrity and fame of Romulus in the estimation of the surrounding nations.

This victory over Acron, and the annexation of his dominions to the Roman commonwealth, are considered of great historical importance, as the original type and exemplar of the whole subsequent foreign policy of the Roman state;—a policy marked by courage and energy in martial action on the field, and by generosity in dealing with the conquered; and which was so successful in its results, that it was the means of extending the Roman power from kingdom to kingdom, and from continent to continent, until the vast organization almost encircled the world.

Romulus faithfully fulfilled the vow which he had made to Jupiter. On the return of the army to Rome, the soldiers, by his directions, cut down a small oak-tree, and trimming the branches at the top, and shortening them as much as was necessary for the purpose, they hung the weapons and armor of Acron upon it, and marched with it thus, in triumph into the city. Romulus walked in the midst of the procession, a crown of laurel upon his head, and his long hair hanging down upon his shoulders. Thus the victors entered the city, greeted all the way by the shouts and acclamations of the people, who had assembled,—men, women, and children,—at the gates and upon the tops of the houses. When the long procession had thus passed in, tables for the soldiers were spread in the streets and public squares, and the whole day was spent in festivity and rejoicing. This was the first Roman triumph,—the original model and example of those magnificent and imposing spectacles which in subsequent ages became the wonder of the world.

The spoils which had been brought in upon the oak were solemnly set up, on one of the hills within the city, as a trophy to Jupiter. A small temple was erected expressly to receive them. This temple was very small, being but five feet wide and ten feet long.

A short time after these transactions two other cities were incorporated into the Roman state. The name of these cities were Crustumenium and Antemnæ. Some women from these cities had been seized at Rome when the Sabine women were taken, and the inhabitants had been ever since that period meditating plans of revenge. They were not strong enough to wage open war against Romulus, but they began at last to make hostile incursions into the Roman territories by means of such small bands of armed men as they had the means of raising. Romulus immediately organized bodies of troops sufficient for the purpose, and then suddenly, and, as it would seem, without giving the kings of these cities any previous warning, he appeared before the walls and captured the cities before the inhabitants had time to recover from their consternation.

He then sent to all the women in Rome who had formerly belonged to these cities, summoning them to appear before him at his public place of audience in the city, and in the presence of the Roman Senate. The women were exceedingly terrified at receiving this summons. They supposed that death or some other terrible punishment, was to be inflicted upon them in retribution for the offenses committed by their countrymen, and they came into the senate-house, hiding their faces in their robes, and crying out with grief and terror. Romulus bid them calm their fears, assuring them that he intended them no injury. "Your countrymen," said he, "preferred war to the peaceful alternative of friendship and alliance which we offered them; and the fortune of war to which they thus chose to appeal, has decided against them. They have now fallen into our hands, and are wholly at our mercy. We do not, however, mean to do them any harm. We spare and forgive them for your sakes. We intend to invite them to come and live with us and with you at Rome, so that you can once more experience the happiness of being joined to your fathers and brothers as well as your husbands. We shall not destroy or even injure their cities; but shall send some of our own citizens to people them, so that they may become fully incorporated into the Roman commonwealth. Thus, your fathers and brothers, and all your countrymen, receive the boon of life, liberty, and happiness through you; and all that we ask of you in return, is that you will continue your conjugal affection and fidelity to your Roman husbands, and seek to promote the harmony and happiness of the city by every means in your power."

Of course such transactions as these attracted great attention throughout the country, and both the valor with which Romulus encountered his enemies while they resisted and opposed him, and the generosity with which he admitted them to an honorable alliance with him when they were reduced to submission, were universally applauded. In fact, there began to be formed a strong public sentiment in favor of the new colony, and the influx to it of individual adventurers, from all parts of the country, rapidly increased. In one instance a famous chieftain named Cælius, a general of the Etrurians who lived north of the Tiber, brought over the whole army under his command in a body, to join the new colony. New and special arrangements were necessary to be made at Rome for receiving so sudden and so large an accession to the numbers of the people, and accordingly a new eminence, one which had been hitherto without the city, was now inclosed, and brought within the pœmerium. This hill received the name of Cælius, from the general whose army occupied it. The city was extended too at the same time on the other side toward the Tiber. The walls were continued down to the very bank of the river, and thence carried along the bank so as to present a continued defense on that side, except at one place where there was a great gate leading to the water.

During all this time, however, the Sabines still cherished the spirit of resentment and hostility, and instead of being conciliated by the forbearance and generosity of the Romans, were only excited to greater jealousy and ill- will at witnessing the proofs of their increasing influence and power. They employed themselves in maturing their plans for a grand onset against the new colony, and with the intention to make the blow which they were about to strike effectual and final they took time to arrange their preparations on the most extensive scale, and to mature them in the most deliberate and thorough manner. They enlisted troops; they collected stores of provisions and munitions of war; they formed alliances with such states lying beyond them as they could draw into their quarrel; and finally, when all things were ready, they assembled their forces upon the frontier, and prepared for the onset. The name of the general who was placed in command of this mighty host was Titus Tatius.

In the mean time, Romulus and the people of the city were equally busy in making preparations for defense. They procured and laid up in magazines, great stores of provisions for the use of the city. They strengthened and extended the walls, and built new ramparts and towers wherever they were needed. Numitor rendered very essential aid to his grandson in these preparations. He sent supplies of weapons to him for the use of the men, and furnished various military engines, such as were used in those times in the attack and defense of besieged cities. In fact, the preparations on both sides were of the most extensive character, and seemed to portend a very resolute and determined contest.

When all things were thus ready, the Sabines, before actually striking the blow for which they had been so long and so deliberately preparing, concluded to send one more final embassy to Romulus, to demand the surrender of the women. This was of course only a matter of form, as they must have known well from what had already passed that Romulus would not now yield to such a proposal. He did not yield. He sent back word in answer to their demand, that the Sabine women were all well settled in Rome, and were contented and happy there with their husbands and friends, and that he could not think now of disturbing them. This answer having been received, the Sabines prepared for the onset.

There was a certain tract of country surrounding Rome which belonged to the people of the city, and was cultivated by them. This land was used partly for tillage and partly for the pasturage of cattle, but principally for the latter, as the rearing of flocks and herds was, for various reasons, a more advantageous mode of procuring food for man in those ancient days than the culture of the ground. The rural population, therefore, of the Roman territory consisted chiefly of herdsmen; and when the approaching danger from the Sabines became imminent, Romulus called all these herdsmen in, and required the flocks of sheep and the herds of cattle to be driven to the rear of the city, and shut up in an inclosure there, where they could be more easily defended. Thus the Sabine army found, when they were ready to cross the frontier, that the Roman territory, on that side, was deserted and solitary; and that there was nothing to oppose them in advancing across it almost to the very gates of Rome.

They advanced accordingly, and when they came near to the city they found that Romulus had taken possession of two hills without the walls, where he had entrenched himself in great force. These two hills were named the Esquiline and Quirinal hills. The city itself included two other hills, namely, the Palatine and the Capitoline. The Capitoline hill was the one on which the asylum had formerly been built, and it was now the citadel. The citadel was surrounded on all parts with ramparts and towers which overlooked and commanded all the neighboring country. The command of this fortress was given to Tarpeius, a noble Roman. He had a daughter named Tarpeia, whose name afterward became greatly celebrated in history, on account of the part which she took in the events of this siege, as will presently appear.

At the foot of the Capitoline hill, and on the western side of it, that is, the side away from the city, there was a spacious plain which was afterward included within the limits of the city, and used as a parade-ground, under the name of Campus Martius, which words mean the "War Field." This field was now, however, an open plain, and the Sabine army advancing to it, encamped upon it. The Sabine forces were much more numerous than those of the Romans, but the latter were so well guarded and protected by their walls and fortifications, that Titus Tatius saw no feasible way of attacking them with any prospect of success. At last, one day as some of his officers were walking around the Capitoline hill, looking at the walls of the citadel, Tarpeia came to one of the gates, which was in a retired and solitary position, and entered into a parley with the men. The story of what followed is variously related by different historians, and it is now difficult to ascertain the actual truth respecting it. The account generally received is this:—

Tarpeia had observed the soldiers from the walls, and her attention had been attracted by the bracelets and rings which they wore; and she finally made an agreement with the Sabines that she would open the postern gate in the night, and let them in, if they would give her what they wore upon their arms, meaning the ornaments which had attracted her attention. The Sabines bound themselves to do this and then went away. Titus Tatius, accordingly, when informed of this arrangement detailed a strong detachment of troops, and gave them orders to repair at night in a very silent and secret manner to the gate which had been designated as the place where they were to be let in. It is asserted, however, by some writers, that this apparent treachery on the part of Tarpeia was only a deep-laid stratagem on her part to draw the Sabines into a snare; and that she sent word to Romulus, informing him of the agreement which she had made, in order that he might secretly dispatch a strong force to take their position at the gate, and intercept and capture the Sabine party as soon as they should come in. But if this was Tarpeia's design, it totally failed. The Sabines, when they came at midnight to the postern gate which Tarpeia opened for them, came in sufficient force to bear down all opposition; and in fulfillment of their promise to give Tarpeia what they wore upon their arms they threw their heavy bucklers upon her until she was crushed down beneath the weight of them and killed.

Promising the Bracelets

A steep rock which forms that side of the Capitoline hill is called the Tarpeian rock, in memory of this maiden, to the present day.

In this way the Sabines gained possession of the citadel, though Romulus still held the main city. The Romans were of course extremely disconcerted at the loss of the citadel, and Romulus, finding that the danger was now extremely imminent, resolved no longer to stand on the defensive, but to come out upon the plain and offer the Sabines battle. He accordingly brought his forces out of the city and took up a strong position with them, between the Capitoline and Palatine hills, with his front toward the Campus Martius, where the main body of the Sabines were posted. Thus the armies were confronted against each other on the plain, the Romans holding the city and the Palatine hill as a stronghold to retreat to in case of necessity, while the Sabines in the same manner could seek refuge on the Capitoline hill and in the citadel.

Things being in this state a series of desperate but partial contests ensued, which were continued for several days, when at length a general battle came on. During all this time the walls of the city and of the citadel were lined with spectators who had ascended to witness the combats; for from these walls and from the declivities of the hills, the whole plain could be looked down upon as if it were a map. The battle continued all day. At night both parties were exhausted, and the field was covered with the dead and dying, but neither side had gained a victory. The next day by common consent they suspended the combat in order to take care of the wounded, and to bury the bodies of the dead.

After the interval of a day, which was spent, on both sides, in removing the horrid relics of the previous combats, and in gathering fresh strength and fresh desperation and rage for the conflicts yet to come, the struggle was renewed. The soldiers fought now, on this renewal of the battle, with more dreadful and deadly ferocity than ever. Various incidents occurred during the day to give one party or the other a local or temporary advantage, but neither side wholly prevailed. At one time Romulus himself was exposed to the most imminent personal danger, and for a time it was thought that he was actually killed. The Romans had gained some great advantage over a party of the Sabines, and the latter were rushing in a headlong flight to the citadel, the Romans pursuing them and hoping to follow them in, in the confusion, and thus regain possession of the fortress. To prevent this, the Sabines within the citadel and on the rocks above threw stones down upon the Romans. One of these stones struck Romulus on the head, and he fell down stunned and senseless under the blow. His men were extremely terrified at this disaster, and abandoning the pursuit of their enemies they took up the body of Romulus and carried it into the city. It was found, however, that he was not seriously injured. He soon recovered from the effects of the blow and returned into the battle.

Another incident which occurred in the course of these battles has been commemorated in history, by having been the means of giving a name to a small lake or pool which was afterward brought within the limits of the city. A Sabine general named Curtius happened at one time to encounter Romulus in a certain part of the field, and a long and desperate combat ensued between the two champions. Other soldiers gradually came up and mingled in the fray, until at length Curtius, finding himself wounded and bleeding, and surrounded by enemies, fled for his life. Romulus pursued him for a short distance, but Curtius at length came suddenly upon a small swampy pool, which was formed of water that had been left by the inundations of the river in some old deserted channel, and which was now covered and almost concealed by some sort of mossy and floating vegetation. Curtius running headlong, and paying little heed to his steps fell into this hole, and sank in the water. Romulus supposed of course that he would be drowned there, and so turned away and went to find some other enemy. Curtius, however, succeeded in crawling out of the pond into which he had fallen; and in commemoration of the incident the pond was named Lake Curtius, which name it retained for centuries afterward, when, not only had all the water disappeared, but the place itself had been filled up, and had been covered with streets and houses.

The combats between the Romans and the Sabines were continued for several days, during all which time the Sabine women, on whose account it was that this dreadful quarrel had arisen, were suffering the greatest anxiety and distress. They loved their fathers and brothers, but then they loved their husbands too; and they were overwhelmed with anguish at the thought that day after day those who were equally dear to them were engaged in fighting and destroying one another, and that they could do nothing to arrest so unnatural a hostility.

At length, however, after suffering extreme distress for many days, a crisis arrived when they found that they could interpose. Both parties had become somewhat weary of the contest. Neither could prevail over the other, and yet neither was willing to yield. The Sabines could not bring themselves to submit to so humiliating an alternative as to withdraw from Rome and leave their daughters and sisters in the captors' hands, after all the grand preparations which they had made for retaking them. And on the other hand the Romans could not take those, who, whatever had been their previous history, were now living happily as wives and mothers, each in her own house in the city, and give them up to an army of invaders, demanding them with threats and violence, without deep dishonor. Thus, though there was a pause in the conflict, and both parties were weary of it, neither was willing to yield, and both were preparing to return to the struggle with new determination and vigor.

The Sabine women thought that they might now interpose. A lady named Hersilia, who is often mentioned as one of the most prominent among the number, proposed this measure and made the arrangements for carrying it into effect. She assembled her country-women and explained to them her plan, which was that they should go in a body to the Roman Senate, and ask permission to intercede between the contending nations, and plead for peace.

The company of women, taking their children with them, all of whom were yet very young, went accordingly in a body to the senate-chamber, and asked to be admitted. The doors were opened to them, and they went in. They all appeared to be in great distress and agitation. The grief and anxiety which they had suffered during the progress of the war still continued, and they begged the Senate to let them go out to the camp of the Sabines, and endeavor to persuade them to make peace. The Senate were disposed to consent. The women wished to take their children with them, but some of the Romans imagined that there might, perhaps, be danger, that under pretense of interceding for peace, they were really intending to make their escape from Rome altogether. So it was insisted that they should leave their children behind them as hostages for their return, excepting that such as had two children were allowed to take one, which plan it was thought would aid them in moving the compassion of their Sabine relatives.

The women, accordingly, left the senate-chamber, and with their children in their arms, their hair disheveled, their robes disordered, and their countenances wan with grief, went in mournful procession out through the gate of the city. They passed across the plain and advanced toward the citadel. They were admitted, and after some delay, were ushered into the council of the Sabines. Here their tears and exclamations of grief broke forth anew. When silence was in some measure restored, Hersilia addressed the Sabine chieftains, saying, that she and her companions had come to beg their countrymen to put an end to the war. "We know," said she, "that you are waging it on our account, and we see in all that you have done proofs of your love for us. In fact, it was our supposed interests which led you to commence it, but now our real interests require that it should be ended. It is true that when we were first seized by the Romans we felt greatly wronged, but having submitted to our fate, we have now become settled in our new homes, and are contented and happy in them. We love our husbands and love our children; and we are treated with the utmost kindness and respect by all. Do not then, under a mistaken kindness for us, attempt to tear us away again, or continue this dreadful war, which, though ostensibly on our account, and for our benefit, is really making us inexpressibly miserable."

This intercession produced the effect which might have been expected from it. The Sabines and Romans immediately entered upon negotiations for peace, and peace is easily made where both parties are honestly desirous of making it. In fact, a great reaction took place, so that from the reckless and desperate hostility which the two nations had felt for each other, there succeeded so friendly a sentiment, that in the end a treaty of union was made between the two nations. It was agreed that the two nations should be merged into one. The Sabine territory was to be annexed to that of Rome, and Titus Tatius, with the principal Sabine chieftains, were to remove to Rome, which was thenceforth to be the capital of the new kingdom. In a word, never was a reconciliation between two belligerent nations so sudden and so complete.

13

The Conclusion

AFTER the termination of the Sabine war, Romulus continued to reign many years, and his reign, although no very exact and systematic history of it was recorded at the time, seems to have presented the usual variety of incidents and vicissitudes; and yet, notwithstanding occasional and partial reverses, the city, and the kingdom connected with it, made rapid progress in wealth and population.

For four or five years after the union of the Sabines with the Romans, Titus Tatius was in some way or other associated with Romulus in the government of the united kingdom. Romulus, during all this time, had his house and his court on the Palatine hill, where the city had been originally built, and where most of the Romans lived. The head-quarters of the Sabine chieftain were, on the other hand, upon the Capitoline hill, which was the place on which the citadel was situated that his troops had taken possession of in the course of the war, and which it seems they continued to occupy after the peace. The space between the two hills was set apart as a market-place, or forum, as it was called in their language,—that place being designated for the purpose on account of its central and convenient situation. When afterward that portion of the city became filled as it did with magnificent streets and imposing architectural edifices, the space which Romulus had set apart for a market remained an open public square, and as it was the scene in which transpired some of the most remarkable events connected with

Roman history, it became renowned throughout the world under the name of the Roman Forum.

In consequence of the union of the Romans and the Sabines, and of the rapid growth of the city in population and power which followed, the Roman state began soon to rise to so high a position in relation to the surrounding cities and kingdoms, as soon to take precedence of them altogether. This was owing, however, in part undoubtedly, to the character of the men who governed at Rome. The measures which they adopted in founding the city, and in sustaining it through the first years of its existence, as described in the foregoing chapters, were all of a very extraordinary character, and evinced very extraordinary qualities in the men who devised them. These measures were bold, comprehensive and sagacious, and they were carried out with a certain combination of courage and magnanimity which always gives to those who possess it, and who are in a position to exercise it on a commanding scale, great ascendency over the minds of men. They who possess these qualities generally feel their power, and are usually not slow to assert it. A singular and striking instance of this occurred not many years after the peace with the Sabines. There was a city at some distance from Rome called Cameria, whose inhabitants were a lawless horde, and occasionally parties of them made incursions, as was said, into the surrounding countries, for plunder. The Roman Senate sent word to the government of the city that such accusations were made against them, and very coolly cited them to appear at Rome for trial. The Camerians of course refused to come. The Senate then declared war against them, and sent an army to take possession of the city, proceeding to act in the case precisely as if the Roman government constituted a judicial tribunal, having authority to exercise jurisdiction, and to enforce law and order, among all the nations around them. In fact, Rome continued to assert and to maintain this authority over a wider and wider circle every year, until in the course of some centuries after Romulus's day, she made herself the arbiter of the world.

Titus Tatius shared the supreme power with Romulus at Rome for several years, and the two monarchs continued during this time to exercise their joint power in a much more harmonious manner than would have been supposed possible. At length, however, causes of disagreement began to occur, and in the end open dissension took place, in the course of which Tatius came to his end in a very sudden and remarkable manner. A party of soldiers from Rome, it seems, had been committing some deed of violence at Lavinium, the ancient city which Æneas had built when he first arrived in Latium. The people of Lavinium complained to Romulus against these marauders. It happened, however, that the guilty men were chiefly Sabines, and in the discussions which took place at Rome afterward in relation to the affair, Tatius took their part, and endeavored to shield them, while Romulus seemed disposed to give them up to the Lavinians for punishment. "They are robbers and murderers," said Romulus, "and we ought not to shield them from the penalty due to their crimes." "They are Roman citizens," said Tatius, "and we must not give them up to a foreign state." The controversy became warm; parties were formed; and at last the exasperation became so great that when the Lavinian envoys, who had come to Rome to demand the punishment of the robbers, were returning home, a gang of Tatius's men intercepted them on the way and killed them.

This of course increased the excitement and the difficulty in a tenfold degree. Romulus immediately sent to Lavinium to express his deep regret at what had occurred, and his readiness to do every thing in his power to expiate the offense which his countrymen had committed. He would arrest these murderers, he said, and send them to Lavinium, and he would come himself, with Tatius, to Lavinium, and there make an expiatory offering to the gods, in attestation of the abhorrence which they both felt for so atrocious a crime as waylaying and murdering the embassadors of a friendly city. Tatius was compelled to assent to these measures, though he yielded very reluctantly. He could not openly defend such a deed as the murder of the envoys; and so he consented to accompany Romulus to Lavinium, to make the offering, but he secretly arranged a plan for rescuing the murderers from the Lavinians, after they had been given up. Accordingly, while he and Romulus were at Lavinium offering the sacrifices, news came that the murderers of the envoys, on their way from Rome to Lavinium, had been rescued and allowed to escape. This news so exasperated the people of Lavinium against Tatius, for they considered him as unquestionably the secret author and contriver of the deed, that they rose upon him at the festival, and murdered him with the butcher knives and spits which had been used for slaughtering and roasting the animals. They then formed a grand procession and escorted Romulus out of the city in safety with loud acclamations.

The government of Lavinium, as soon as the excitement of the scene was over, fearing the resentment which they very naturally supposed Romulus would feel at the murder of his colleague, seized the ringleaders of the riot, and sent them bound to Rome, to place them at the disposal of the Roman government. Romulus sent them back unharmed, directing them to say to the Lavinian government, that he considered the death of Tatius, though inflicted in a mode lawless and unjustifiable, as nevertheless, in itself, only a just expiation for the murder of the Lavinian embassadors, which Tatius had instigated or authorized.

The Sabines of Rome were for a time greatly exasperated at these occurrences, but Romulus succeeded in gradually quieting and calming them, and they finally acquiesced in his decision. Romulus thus became once more the sole and undisputed master of Rome.

After this the progress of the city in wealth and prosperity, from year to year, was steady and sure, interrupted, it is true, by occasional and temporary reverses, but with no real retrocession at any time. Causes of disagreement arose from time to time with neighboring states, and, in such cases, Romulus always first sent a summons to the party implicated, whether king or people, citing them to appear and answer for their conduct before the Roman Senate. If they refused to come, he sent an armed force against them, as if he were simply enforcing the jurisdiction of a tribunal of justice. The result usually was that the refractory state was compelled to submit, and its territories were added to those of the kingdom of Rome. Thus the boundaries of the new empire were widening and extending every year.

Romulus paid great attention, in the mean time, to every thing pertaining to the internal organization of the state, so as to bring every part of the national administration into the best possible condition. The municipal police, the tribunals of justice, the social institutions and laws of the industrial classes, the discipline of the troops, the enlargement and increase of the fortifications of the city, and the supply of arms, and stores, and munitions of war,—and every other subject, in fact, connected with the welfare and prosperity of the city,—occupied his thoughts in every interval of peace and tranquility. In consequence of the exertions which he made, and the measures which he adopted, order and system prevailed more and more in every department, and the community became every year better organized, and more and more consolidated; so that the capacity of the city to receive accessions to the population increased even faster than accessions were made. In a word, the solid foundations were laid of that vast superstructure, which, in subsequent ages, became the wonder of the world.

Notwithstanding, however, all this increasing greatness and prosperity, Romulus was not without rivals and enemies, even among his own people at Rome. The leading senators became, at last, envious and jealous of his power. They said that he himself grew imperious and domineering in spirit, as he grew older, and manifested a pride and haughtiness of demeanor which excited their ill-will. He assumed too much authority, they said, in the management of public affairs, as if he were an absolute and despotic sovereign. He wore a purple robe on public occasions, as a badge of royalty. He organized a body-guard of three hundred young troopers, who rode before him whenever he moved about the city; and in all respects assumed such pomp and parade in his demeanor, and exercised such a degree of arbitrary power in his acts, as made him many enemies. The whole Senate became, at length, greatly disaffected.

At last one day, on occasion of a great review which took place at a little distance from the city, there came up a sudden shower, attended with thunder and lightning, and the violence of the tempest was such as to compel the soldiers to retire precipitately from the ground in search of some place of shelter. Romulus was left with a number of senators who were at that time attending upon him, alone, on the shore of a little lake which was near the place that had been chosen for the parade. After a short time the senators themselves came away from the ground, and returned to the city; but Romulus was not with them. The story which they told was that in the middle of the tempest, Romulus had been suddenly enveloped in a flame which seemed to come down in a bright flash of lightning from the clouds, and immediately afterward had been taken up in the flame to heaven.

The Death of Romulus

This strange story was but half believed even at first, by the people, and very soon rumors began to circulate in the city that Romulus had been murdered by the senators who were around him at the time of the shower,—they having seized the occasion afforded by the momentary absence of his guards, and by their solitary position. There were various surmises in respect to the disposal which the assassins had made of the body. The most obvious supposition was that it had been sunk in the lake. There was, however, a horrible report circulated that the senators had disposed of it by cutting it up into small pieces, and conveying it away, each taking a portion, under their robes.

Of course these rumors produced great agitation and excitement throughout the city. The current of public sentiment set strongly against the senators. Still as nothing could be positively ascertained in respect to the transaction, the mystery seemed to grow more dark and dreadful every day, and the public mind was becoming more and more deeply agitated. At length, however, the mystery was suddenly explained by a revelation, which, whatever may be thought of it at the present day, was then entirely satisfactory to the whole community.

One of the most prominent and distinguished of the senators, named Proculus, one who it seems had not been present among the other senators in attendance upon Romulus at the time when he disappeared, came forward one day before a grand assembly which had been convened for the purpose, and announced to them in the most solemn manner, that the spirit of Romulus had appeared to him in a visible form, and had assured him that the story which the other senators had told of the ascension of their chieftain to heaven in a flame of fire was really true. "I was journeying," said Proculus, "in a solitary place, when Romulus appeared to me. At first I was exceedingly terrified. The form of the vision was taller than that of a mortal man, and it was clothed in armor of the most resplendent brightness. As soon as I had in some measure recovered my composure I spoke to it. 'Why,' said I, 'have you left us so suddenly? and especially why did you leave us at such a time, and in such a way, as to bring suspicion and reproach on the Roman senators?' 'I left you,' said he, 'because it pleased the gods to call me back again to heaven, whence I originally came. It was no longer necessary for me to remain on earth, for Rome is now established, and her future greatness and glory are sure. Go back to Rome and communicate this to the people. Tell them that if they continue industrious, virtuous, and brave, the time will come when their city will be the mistress of the world; and that I, no longer its king, am henceforth to be its tutelar divinity.'"

The people of Rome were overjoyed to hear this communication. Their doubts and suspicions were now all removed; the senators at once recovered their good standing in the public regard, and all was once more peace and harmony. Altars were immediately erected to Romulus, and the whole population of the city joined in making sacrifices and in paying other divine honors to his memory.

The declaration of Proculus that he had seen the spirit of Romulus, and his report of the conversation which the spirit had addressed to him, constituted proof of the highest kind, according to the ideas which prevailed in those ancient days. In modern times, however, there is no faith in such a story, and the truth in respect to the end of Romulus can now never be known.

After the death of Romulus the senators undertook to govern the State themselves, holding the supreme power one by one, in regular rotation. This plan was, however, not found to succeed, and after an interregnum of about a year, the people elected another king.

THE END

ABOUT JACOB ABBOTT

Jacob Abbott was born in Hallowell, Maine in 1803, the son of a minister and farmer. Even as a young boy, he showed academic promise and an interest in spiritual matters. After attending the Hallowell Academy, he was admitted to Bowdoin College at the age of 14.

At Bowdoin, Abbott studied classics and mathematics. He graduated second in his class in 1820 at the young age of 16. He was known as a serious and studious young man who strove for excellence.

After college, Abbott went on to study at Andover Theological Seminary with the intention of becoming a Congregationalist minister. However, his rigorous study habits and frail health caused him to abandon this pursuit after just two years.

Abbott was plagued by gastrointestinal issues and migraines throughout his life, likely exacerbated by the demanding academic environment. His poor health finally forced him to leave his ministerial studies and turn to the less stressful pursuits of writing and tutoring.

First, Abbott took a job as a professor of mathematics and natural philosophy at Amherst College in 1824. The following year, he married Harriet Vaughan and moved to Boston where he opened a school for young ladies. It was during this time that he began writing simple textbooks for teaching science, history and Christian values.

So while Abbott had aspired to be a minister, chronic health issues led him to find an alternate calling educating children through clear and engaging writing. This pivot would launch his successful career as one of the most famous children's authors of the 19th century.

In 1825, Abbott married Harriet Vaughan and soon after started his own school for young ladies in Boston. During this time, he began

ABOUT JACOB ABBOTT

writing educational books in a popular, simple style. His early works included the Mount Vernon Reader and The Young Christian.

Abbott gained fame with the Rollo series, first published in 1835. These stories followed a young boy named Rollo learning morals and virtues through his everyday adventures. The series was hugely popular and established Abbott's reputation as a gifted children's writer.

Other notable books by Abbott include the Franconia Stories (1853-1873), a 10-volume series about a brother and sister's adventures in the country, and the Marco Paul series (1853-1873), which followed a boy's travels around America learning about each state.

In all, Jacob Abbott wrote over 200 books, primarily for young readers. His works were praised for their ability to educate and impart moral lessons in an engaging, story-driven way. Though largely forgotten today, he was one of the most prolific and beloved children's authors of his era.

Abbott continued writing up until his death on October 31, 1879 in Farmington, Maine. His legacy lives on through his contributions to 19th century children's literature.

BIOGRAPHIES BY JACOB ABBOTT

A number of the books Abbott wrote were biographies of famous people. Famous characters covered in these books included:

Alexander the Great: This book provides a sweeping look at the life and achievements of Alexander III of Macedon, better known as Alexander the Great. It follows his early education by Aristotle, ascension to the throne after his father Philip II's assassination, and extensive military campaigns across Asia and northeast Africa. Abbott recounts Alexander's major battles against the Persians and annexation of their empire. The book also examines Alexander's tactics, military innovations, and creation of a Hellenistic empire stretching from Greece to India before his death at 32.

Alfred the Great: This biography focuses on Alfred's defense of the Kingdom of Wessex against Viking raids in 9th century England. It discusses how Alfred drove back the Great Heathen Army and then negotiated terms with the Vikings, designating parts of England for their settlement. Abbott also highlights Alfred's efforts to revive learning and education in England, as well as his codification of laws and strengthening of the Anglo-Saxon navy. The book frames Alfred as a scholarly, strategic and devout ruler whose achievements laid the foundation for a unified England.

King Charles I: This book looks at the reign of Charles I leading up to and during the English Civil War. It focuses on the religious and political conflicts between Charles I and Parliament, caused largely by

Charles' belief in divine right of kings and many unpopular, authoritarian policies. Abbott also examines Charles' refusal to compromise, leading to the war against Parliament's New Model Army and his eventual execution for treason in 1649 under Oliver Cromwell.

King Charles II: This biography deals with the restoration of the English monarchy under Charles II after the death of Oliver Cromwell. It follows Charles II's return from exile and re-establishment of royal power. However, Abbott also notes Charles' own conflicts with Parliament and religious controversies during his reign. The book discusses Charles' hedonistic lifestyle and many mistresses, but also his support for science, exploration and trade that helped expand the British Empire.

Cleopatra: This book examines Cleopatra VII's life and rule over ancient Egypt. Abbott chronicles Cleopatra's relationships and political alliances with Julius Caesar and Mark Antony, as she sought to maintain Egypt's independence from Rome. The biography highlights Cleopatra's intelligence, education and strategic skills in dealing with Rome. But it ultimately focuses on Cleopatra's downfall and suicide after Mark Antony's defeat by Octavian, leading to Egypt becoming a Roman province.

Cyrus the Great: This biography covers Cyrus II of Persia, founder of the Achaemenid Empire. Abbott traces Cyrus's rise from Persian prince, to revolt against the Medes, to conqueror of the Lydian and Babylonian empires. The book also examines Cyrus's leadership qualities and tolerant policies toward conquered peoples. It portrays Cyrus as a wise, inspirational leader who created the model of a centralized Persian state.

Darius: This book looks at the reign of Darius I, examining his consolidation of the Persian Empire through administrative reforms, development of infrastructure, and expansion of territory. Abbott discusses

Darius's división of the empire into provinces and implementation of a uniform tax system and coinage. The biography also covers his invasion of Greece which was thwarted at the famous Battle of Marathon. Overall, it presents Darius as an capable, pragmatic ruler under whom the Persian Empire reached its zenith.

Queen Elizabeth: This biography celebrates the long and prosperous reign of Queen Elizabeth I of England. Abbott focuses on Elizabeth's shrewd leadership, religious compromise, and patronage of the arts and literature that fostered English Renaissance culture. The book also highlights Elizabeth's naval defeat of the Spanish Armada which secured England's independence from Europe. Overall, Abbott portrays Elizabeth as a commanding, canny and popular female ruler who strengthened England as a major world power.

Genghis Khan: This book looks at the incredible rise of Temüjin, better known as Genghis Khan. It follows his hardships as an outcast youth to becoming the fearsome founder of the Mongol Empire. Abbott chronicles Genghis Khan's brilliant military tactics and utterly ruthless conquests that allowed the Mongols to dominate much of Asia and Eastern Europe. Overall it paints him as a complex figure--strategic genius but also brutal tyrant.

Hannibal: This biography focuses on the great Carthaginian general Hannibal Barca. It recounts his famous crossing of the Alps with war elephants and invasion of Italy during the Second Punic War against Rome. Abbott details Hannibal's victories in major battles like Cannae but also his eventual defeat by Scipio and exile. The book celebrates Hannibal's daring military prowess but also concession late in life that Rome could not be conquered.

Josephine: This book examines the life of Josephine Bonaparte from her aristocratic upbringing in Martinique to her marriage to Napoleon Bonaparte. It focuses on Josephine's time as Empress consort of France and her support for arts and education. But it also discusses Napoleon's eventual divorce from her due to dynastic pressures. Overall the book presents Josephine as an intelligent, compassionate woman who tempered some of Napoleon's ambition.

Julius Caesar: This traces Caesar's life from early military campaigns to dictator and eventual assassination. Abbott covers Caesar's conquest of Gaul, rivalry with Pompey, famously crossing the Rubicon and crowning as dictator. The biography also examines the conspiracy led by Brutus and Cassius to assassinate Caesar in order to save the Roman Republic. In all, the book presents Caesar as an unmatched military mind who irrevocably changed the Roman Empire.

Margaret of Anjou: This biography looks at Margaret of Anjou who became queen consort to England's King Henry VI. It focuses on the political intrigue and machinations Margaret became involved in to support her husband's reign during the War of the Roses. Abbott portrays Margaret as a fiercely devoted, cunning woman who backed the Lancastrians against factions like the Yorkists led by Richard Neville. Though she lost power, the book frames her as a dominant figure during the conflict.

Mary, Queen of Scots: This book examines the life of Mary Stuart who became Queen of Scotland as an infant. It follows her tumultuous reign marked by scandals and plots to overthrow her by Protestants. Her Catholicism also put her at odds with England's Elizabeth I. Abbott recounts Mary's forced abdication, escape to England, and eventual execution ordered by Elizabeth for plotting against her. Overall it presents a tragic figure whose life was marked by political and religious turmoil.

Nero: This biography looks at the notorious Roman emperor Nero. It explores his self-indulgent lifestyle and tyrannical rule marked by possible matricide and the brutal execution of Christians. Abbott also examines legends around Nero like his fiddling during the Great Fire of Rome. The book presents a despotic, unstable man who drastically weakened the Roman Empire.

Peter the Great: This book covers the reforms and policies of Peter the Great that rapidly westernized Russia. Abbott discusses Peter's extensive European travels as a youth and later programs to remake Russia's army, expand its naval fleet, and build a new capital in St. Petersburg. The biography also examines Peter's harsh, authoritarian approach to governing that consolidated his power. Overall it presents him as a pivotal, transformative tsar.

Pyrrhus: This examines the life and military exploits of Pyrrhus, king of Epirus. It focuses on his campaigns against Rome where he won major battles but suffered heavy losses, giving rise to the term "Pyrrhic victory." Abbott recounts Pyrrhus's struggles to build a Greek empire and failed invasion of Sicily against Carthage. Though a skilled commander, Pyrrhus ultimately failed to achieve lasting gains.

Richard I: This biography looks at the reign of Richard I, known as Lionheart. It focuses on Richard's leadership during the Third Crusade to recapture Jerusalem from Saladin. Abbott also details the legendary tales of Richard's bravery and valor in campaigns against France and during his imprisonment. Overall, the book presents Richard I as one of England's great warrior kings.

Richard II: This explores the reign and overthrow of King Richard II. Abbott covers Richard's despotic actions that led the nobles to revolt and install Henry IV, leading to Richard's imprisonment and likely murder. The biography presents a weak king whose tyranny and poor leadership during a peasant's revolt cost him power and his life.

Richard III: This delves into the controversial rule of Richard III. Abbott examines Richard's contested path to the throne and the disappearance of the Princes in the Tower which Richard likely ordered. It also portrays Richard's defeat at the hands of Henry Tudor at the Battle of Bosworth Field that ended the Wars of the Roses. Ultimately Abbott paints Richard III as willing to employ any means to gain and retain the English crown.

Romulus: This recounts the Roman legend of Romulus and Remus, twin brothers raised by a she-wolf who went on to found the city of Rome. Abbott covers the myths of the brothers' quarrel over leadership, with Romulus killing Remus and becoming Rome's first king and architect of its nascent political institutions. Though mythological, Romulus represents ancient Rome's founding origins and rise to power.

William the Conqueror: This biography follows William, Duke of Normandy's conquest of England in 1066 after victory at the Battle of Hastings. Abbott discusses William's reign as king where he consolidated control, introduced feudalism, and fused English and Norman culture. William is presented as a formidable, innovative Norman leader who irrevocably transformed Anglo-Saxon England.

Xerxes: This examines the reign of Xerxes I of Persia, known for his failed invasion of Greece. Abbott focuses on Xerxes's gathering of a massive army to crush Greek resistance, but defeat at Salamis ended his ambitions. The book covers later unrest and palace intrigue that clouded the end of Xerxes's reign. Overall he is portrayed as a rash ruler whose desire for conquest led to disaster for Persia.

www.ingramcontent.com/pod-product-compliance
Lightning Source LLC
Chambersburg PA
CBHW070101080526
44586CB00013B/1146